People who Changed
the Course of History

Leonardo da Vinci

500 YEARS AFTER HIS DEATH

by Antone Pierucci
Foreword by Dr. Ross King

PEOPLE WHO CHANGED THE COURSE OF HISTORY: LEONARDO DA VINCI 500 YEARS AFTER HIS DEATH

1405 SW 6th Avenue • Ocala, Florida 34471 • Phone 800-814-1132 • Fax 352-622-1875
Website: www.atlantic-pub.com • Email: sales@atlantic-pub.com
SAN Number: 268-1250

Library of Congress Cataloging-in-Publication Data

Names: Pierucci, Antone R. E., author.
Title: People that changed the course of history : the story of Leonardo da Vinci 500 years after his death / Antone Pierucci.
Description: Ocala, Florida : Atlantic Publishing Group, Inc., 2017. | Includes bibliographical references and index.
Identifiers: LCCN 2017045537 (print) | LCCN 2017046614 (ebook) | ISBN 9781620234266 (ebook) | ISBN 9781620234259 (pbk. : alk. paper) | ISBN 9781620234242 (hardcover : alk. paper) | ISBN 1620234254 (alk. paper)
Subjects: LCSH: Leonardo, da Vinci, 1452-1519. | Artists—Italy—Biography.
Classification: LCC N6923.L33 (ebook) | LCC N6923.L33 P548 2017 (print) | DDC 709.2 [B]—dc23
LC record available at https://lccn.loc.gov/2017045537

Printed in the United States

PROJECT MANAGER: Danielle Lieneman
INTERIOR LAYOUT: Nicole Sturk

Reduce. Reuse.
RECYCLE.

A decade ago, Atlantic Publishing signed the Green Press Initiative. These guidelines promote environmentally friendly practices, such as using recycled stock and vegetable-based inks, avoiding waste, choosing energy-efficient resources, and promoting a no-pulping policy. We now use 100-percent recycled stock on all our books. The results: in one year, switching to post-consumer recycled stock saved 24 mature trees, 5,000 gallons of water, the equivalent of the total energy used for one home in a year, and the equivalent of the greenhouse gases from one car driven for a year.

Over the years, we have adopted a number of dogs from rescues and shelters. First there was Bear and after he passed, Ginger and Scout. Now, we have Kira, another rescue. They have brought immense joy and love not just into our lives, but into the lives of all who met them.

We want you to know a portion of the profits of this book will be donated in Bear, Ginger and Scout's memory to local animal shelters, parks, conservation organizations, and other individuals and nonprofit organizations in need of assistance.

– Douglas & Sherri Brown,
President & Vice-President of Atlantic Publishing

Table of Contents

Foreword

Is there anyone in history more fascinating than Leonardo da Vinci? He was brilliant at almost everything. Besides painting some of the world's most famous works of art, he was a visionary inventor who kept imagining how our lives could be made better. He dreamed of flying 400 years before Orville and Wilbur Wright took to the air at Kitty Hawk. He made discoveries in anatomy so far in advance of their time that, 500 years later, his drawings have helped a surgeon in England understand how to repair heart valves. His design for a robot even inspired the work of a roboticist working for NASA. There seems to be nothing to which he couldn't turn his hand or brain.

However, one of the most intriguing and unexpected things about Leonardo is that he struggled throughout his life with failures and disappointments. He didn't, in fact, succeed at everything. Success didn't come early to him. He was what we might call a late bloomer. He had achieved so little by his mid-30s that a poet mocked him by saying he had barely managed to complete a painting in 10 years. That insult must have stung because in a way it was true. However, he left work unfinished not because of laziness but because he was a perfectionist who studied problems and designs from every conceivable angle. Genius, he knew, takes time and effort.

Leonardo was in his 30s before he completed what would later be considered his first masterpiece, *The Virgin of the Rocks*, now in the Louvre in

Paris. That was a late start considering that Michelangelo, before he reached his 30th birthday, had sculpted both the *Pietà* (in Rome) and the gigantic *David* (in Florence). But *The Virgin of the Rocks* failed to bring Leonardo the fame it should have. The men who commissioned it rejected it, and so for many years it sat unseen in Leonardo's studio, the subject of an ugly legal dispute. This failure must have been frustrating for a man who wanted to create what he called a "work of fame." He once wrote down in one of his notebooks a long quotation from Dante's *Inferno*: 'He who, without Fame, burns his life to waste / leaves no more vestige of himself on earth than / wind-blown smoke, or foam upon the water."

Leonardo suffered a number of other disappointments. He hoped to cast a set of bronze doors for the cathedral in the city of Piacenza. However, he was passed over for the job. Another failed attempt was his foray into what today we would call urban planning. He wanted to redevelop Milan so that it had pedestrianized zones, irrigated gardens and even, to cut down on smell and disease, hygienic washrooms. But he failed to get that commission too. He could almost be the patron saint of failed job applications. He even wrote an anonymous reference letter for himself, declaring: "There is no capable man—and you may believe me—except Leonardo the Florentine." That took some nerve.

Then there was the time that Leonardo, together with Niccolò Machiavelli, a politician and writer, devised a plan to reroute the Arno River so that it would bypass Pisa, cutting off this enemy city from the sea — a feat of hydraulic engineering that came to nothing. "How great a distance there is," the historian Francesco Guicciardini observed of these efforts, "between planning things and putting them in operation."

Worst of all, though, was the bronze horse. The Duke of Milan, Ludovico Sforza, hired Leonardo to cast an enormous bronze equestrian monument to glorify Ludovico's father Francesco. However, after almost 10 years of work, this project, which would have made his reputation far and wide as the world's greatest sculptor, was canceled. A war had erupted on the Italian peninsula, and so Leonardo's 75 tons of bronze was shipped away to Ferrara to be turned into cannons. We can imagine him standing on the banks of a canal in Milan, watching his dreams float away on a barge. He was 42 years old at that point, and he must have felt that his name was destined to become nothing more than smoke on the wind or foam on the water.

A phrase often appears in Leonardo's notebooks: "Tell me if I ever did a thing." Leonardo's reach certainly seems to have exceeded his grasp. He wanted to do everything, to know everything. His notebooks are filled with memos about books he hoped to read and people he wished to question or experiments he wished to carry out. If he were alive today, he'd probably be a physicist working on a "theory of everything," trying to link together all known facts of the universe. But he was also interested in obscure facts. His curiosity was insatiable. "Ask Benedetto Portinari," one of his notes reads, "how the people go on the ice in Flanders." Another reminder to himself says: "Inflate the lungs of a pig and observe whether they increase in width and in length, or in width diminishing in length." That was Leonardo— fascinated by both ice-skaters and the size of a pig's lungs. Anyone who met him on the street or in the piazza could expect a grilling. If he could time-travel to us today, he would ask us how cellphones work, how cars run, and most of all, I suspect, how airplanes stay in the air.

Of course, Leonardo was no failure, and those setbacks he did suffer were probably crucial to his many successes. When he lost the commission to cast the bronze horse, he received a different task: to paint the wall in a room in a convent where a band of friars ate their meals. It must have seemed like a comedown, but of course the work that he painted on the wall was *The Last Supper*, one of the world's most famous works of art.

Leonardo had finally, at the age of 46, left a "vestige of himself" for all the world to celebrate.

Leonardo's legacy to us is therefore more than robots, flying machines and even his brilliant artistic masterpieces. It is the proof of the value of perseverance and persistence — the proof that even one of the world's greatest geniuses could triumph despite, or even because of, his self-doubt and insecurities.

—Dr. Ross King

Ross King is the author of many books on art, artists and history. He has written two books on Leonardo da Vinci: *Leonardo and The Last Supper* is about the four years Leonardo spent painting his famous mural in Milan; and *The Fantasia of Leonardo da Vinci* is a collection of the artist's fables, jokes and riddles. Another of his books, *Brunelleschi's Dome*, tells the incredible story of the building of the massive dome of the cathedral in Florence. He has also written books on French Impressionism, including *Mad Enchantment: Claude Monet and the Painting of the Water Lilies*. When not writing, he spends his time traveling with his wife, and giving talks in the United States, England, and Italy.

Introduction

Under the shadow of the immense stone walls of the city of Florence, a cart rattled to a full stop. The young boy in the back of the cart had spent the last hour marveling at the cityscape — each passing minute bringing robust fortification towers, domed palaces, and the peaked belfries of churches into clearer focus. Although now hidden by the pale-yellow walls that surrounded this city of commerce, the young boy could hear the hustle and bustle of the 50,000 people inside. A sharp cry from above called the boy's attention to a kite, a small bird of prey that was gliding on the warm Tuscan wind. Its shadow passed over his upturned face. He loved birds; or, more to the point, they fascinated him.

The young teenager's journey had started some 30 miles away, in the small country town of Vinci. He had certainly visited the city of Florence before — after all, his father was a well-to-do bureaucrat in the city. This visit, however, was entirely different from the previous ones. This time, he had come to stay.

The cart waited behind a line of other carts outside of the city gate. With a flap of its wings, the kite passed from the boy's view over the walls and into the city of Florence. After checking in with the tax collector and the guards posted at the gate (an immense entryway called the Porta San Friano), the cart carrying the curly-haired youth continued on its way as the deeply-rutted dirt path suddenly gave way to a paved street. Soon, that street led over an arched bridge that spanned the Arno River, which cut the city of Florence in two. Clattering over the Ponte alla Carraia, as the bridge was called, the young boy could look down into the sluggish water of the Arno. Rivers entered cities clear and blue and exited them full of trash, human waste, and other unpleasant debris. Florence may have been at the forefront of the age of the Renaissance, but it was still a medieval city.

On its way to the heart of the city, the cart passed by people from all corners of the known world: pale-faced mercenaries from faraway England, swarthy merchants from Greece, turbaned scholars from Egypt, and many more. Florence in the middle of the 15th century may have been a city physically located in northern Italy, but its influence spread across the globe.

When the cart came to a stop, the young boy prepared himself to take the first step of his new life. Behind him was his childhood — the green hills, quiet rivers, and deep woods that had characterized his existence up until then. Now, before him, was a world of art, courtly intrigue, and uncertainty. With resolution, the young Leonardo da Vinci stepped off the cart and into his future.

Renaissance Italy at about 1494 AD — {{PD-1923}}

CHAPTER 1

The World of Leonardo

Leonardo's entrance into Florence at the early age of 14 was an important milestone for him. In his lifetime, he would be many things: an artist, an engineer, a philosopher, and a scientist. History would remember him as the first Renaissance man — a genius of many talents. Despite Leonardo's reputation, he was a man who finished relatively few projects during his four-decade long career.

As an artist, many of his most famous pieces were never actually delivered to the people who paid for them. At times, he didn't even finish a piece before moving onto another. At other times he kept the completed artwork until the client paid him more money he thought he was due. As an engineer, Leonardo rarely built a working machine for a client, instead preferring to doodle extraordinary plans for these things in his notebooks. As a scientist, he never cured any patients or taught at a school, but he certainly dissected enough animals and human cadavers to become more knowledgeable about human anatomy than any living man of his time. He was a doer, a thinker, a lover, an entrepreneur, and a landowner who brushed shoulders with princes and popes, paupers and prostitutes. He was an Italian who died in France, an illegitimate son but never a father himself (that we know of).

How on earth do we begin to untangle the mystery of this man? Well, like us all, Leonardo was both uniquely an individual and a general product of the world into which he was born. Before we can understand the life of this brilliant man and appreciate his work, we must first learn some of the complexities of his world. So, let's start at the beginning.

WHAT'S IN A NAME?

Born during the night of April 15, 1452, in a small country cottage outside the town of Vinci, Italy, Leonardo came into a world very foreign to our own. His full legal name was Leonardo di Ser Piero d'Antonio di Ser Piero di Ser Guido da Vinci. We'll just call him Leonardo da Vinci. Knowing his full legal name is important, though, because built into it is an amazing amount of information about his family. And what better way to learn about the history of Leonardo's world than through his immediate ancestors?

Leonardo is obviously his first name, and a pretty common one for the day, too. The "di Ser Piero" following his first name tells us that Leonardo was the son of Ser Piero ("di" means "of" or "from"). Following this same formula tells us that Ser Piero was son of Antonio, who was son of another Ser Piero, who was son of Ser Guido — all of whom were born in the town of Vinci. Not only do we now have a list of Leonardo's ancestors going back to his great-great-grandfather, Ser Guido, but we also know a little about the social status of the individual men, too.[1]

The word "Ser" is a lot like our English word "sir," but in 14th and 15th century Italy, it was only given to specific classes of men, including those who worked as lawyers or government bureaucrats. From other sources, we know that in the case of the da Vinci men, they worked as notaries. Or, rather, all of them did except Leonardo's grandfather, Antonio, who does not have the title of "Ser" in front of his name. Breaking away from the

---

1. Brockwell, Maurice Walter. *Leonardo Da Vinci*. London: T.C & E.C. Jack, 1908. Electronic. 16.

family tradition of bureaucratic work, Antonio led a somewhat mysterious life, one that his own son and Leonardo's father, Piero, rejected. It is probably no coincidence that Antonio and his other son, Francesco, would play a more significant role in the young Leonardo's life than his own father.

Fun Fact

Notaries were very important people in 14th and 15th century Italy. They were responsible for writing business and legal contracts and overseeing the creation of wills and other such documents. In a culture that thrived on business deals, a notary was a vital part of making the whole machine of state run smoothly.

THE DA VINCI IN FLORENTINE SOCIETY: POSH OR NOT?

Starting with Ser Guido da Vinci and continuing through to Leonardo's father, Ser Piero, the da Vinci family was of good stock. They were never especially wealthy, nor did they ever marry into nobility, but the da Vinci name was a good one, and that mattered in 14th-century Italy. Although we don't know when Ser Guido was born, we know that by 1339 he was already an established notary working with clients in Florence just 30 miles away from his home town of Vinci.[2]

As notaries, the da Vinci were part of the middle class of Florentine society, alongside skilled laborers, artisans and minor merchants. Neither extravagantly wealthy nor from noble families, members of the middle class in Florence weren't impoverished either. Those of the upper class, on the other hand, were extravagantly wealthy. To this group of people belonged the wealthy merchants and craftsmen as well as the nobles. What distinguished

2. Bramly, Serge. *Leonardo: The Artist and the Man.* London: Penguin, 1994. Print, 33

a nobleman from every other member of the upper class was not wealth, but family lineage. The nobles came from powerful and (sometimes) wealthy, landowning families. During the time of Leonardo's ancestors, it was more prestigious to be from a long line of power than a newly-made man of wealth. To the nobles, the wealthy merchants of the upper class were upstarts who came from working families. Hardly the stuff of repute.

In order to distinguish themselves from these newly-rich merchants, the nobles made much about the virtues of knighthood. Although they did occasionally ride into battle, Florentine knights shouldn't be confused with actual knights. Instead, to the nobles, knighthood was more about the ceremony and pomp: the armor, the steed, the lance, and the romanticism around faithful service to the city. All the shiny outfits and courtly balls associated with knighthood marked them as distinctly better — so the nobles thought at least — than the merchants.[3]

Don't Just Take my Word for It!

One of the character's in Niccolò Machiavelli's play set in 15th century Florence highlights the importance of power in the city when he says, "The fact is, if you're one of us and you're not in power, then you won't even find a dog to bark at you!"

Apparently, even the dogs in Florence cared about your status![4]

As an artist and so much more, Leonardo himself remained part of the middle class, even though he frequently brushed elbows with the elite.

---

3. Najemy, John N. A History of Florence: 1200-1575. Massachusetts: Blackwell. 2008. Print, 35.
4. Machiavelli, Niccolo. *Mandragola*. Translated by Nerida Newbigin, Maryland: The Johns Hopkins UP, 2009, 12.

Contact between the classes was actually quite common. Both the upper and middle classes were members of city guilds.

Guilds were organizations created by and for people who worked in specific industries. There were guilds for bookkeepers, bankers, bakers and many others besides.[5] Although in the beginning, most guilds consisted of middle class workers, that didn't last long. By the time Leonardo went to apprentice in Florence in the middle of the 1400s, the guilds had become vehicles of power, with members of the upper class hijacking them for their own purposes.[6]

Although there was a strict distinction between the upper and middle classes in Italian urban society (even when they were members of the same guild), the classes still depended on each other. The upper class depended on everyone below them like any ruler depends on the working class to build structures and produce products to sell. For their part, the nobles and wealthy merchants became the patrons of the arts. They were the consumers, along with the Catholic Church, of all the art and grandeur of the Renaissance. Without the wealthy elite as patrons, artists like Leonardo da Vinci would not have been possible.

THE MAKING OF LEONARDO'S FLORENCE

When Leonardo's great-great-grandfather Ser Guido was working, Florence had already been an established republic for some time. As a republic, the city and surrounding countryside were under the control of a ruling supreme council of men elected from wealthy and sometimes noble families. In Florence, the name of this council was the Signoria. In the early

---

5. Najemy, John N. *A History of Florence: 1200-1575*. Massachusetts: Blackwell, 2008. Print, 43-44.

6. Cohn, Samuel Kline. *The Laboring Classes in Renaissance Florence*. New York: Academic Press, 1980. Print, 136-154.

years, every male resident of Florence had the potential to be elected to the Signoria, but that didn't last very long. Soon, only the wealthy and noble were electable to the governing council, with a few exceptions. What started as a republic soon became an oligarchy — rule by a select few.

In other Italian cities, a form of monarchy replaced the oligarchic supreme council. In these towns, like Milan, a single man led the council. He was called the *signore* or Duke (not to be confused with the entire ruling council of Florence, the Signoria). The title and authority of the individual *signore* was hereditary, meaning it passed down to the eldest son, essentially like the title of king did in other kingdoms.

The creation of these independent city-states, ruled by either a council or an individual duke, made northern Italy a land of many small kingdoms. Each of these kingdoms constantly warred with the others. By the time the da Vinci family made it onto the historical record, the major powers in Italy were the Kingdom of Naples in the south, the pope in Rome, and the cities of Milan, Florence, Venice, and Genoa to the north. There were also smaller cities that held some power, like Urbino and Siena. With constant internal feuding, larger powers outside of Italy frequently interfered, hoping to gain control as well. The most troublesome of these foreign kingdoms during Leonardo's life would be the Kingdom of France.

It was in this world of feuding cities and kingdoms that the da Vinci family entered the scene. The small town of Vinci was located within the influence of the city of Florence. The triumphs and failures of Florence, then, affected the da Vinci family the most. From the time of Ser Guido through the life of Leonardo himself, the city of Florence rejected the monarchic position of a duke. Instead, they preferred to be ruled through the wealthy and noble families of the Signoria. Unfortunately, giving equal power to a small group of people was a recipe for civil war, and 14th-century Florence during the time of Ser Guido and his descendants was rife with feuds.[7]

Fun Fact

Renaissance literally means "rebirth." It is a term used to describe the period of cultural growth that happened in Europe from the mid-14th century to the 17th century (1350 — 1600s). During this time, artistic endeavors took on a new look as philosophy and other types of thought looked with fresh eyes at the ancient Romans and Greeks. The rigid class structure of medieval society — with serfs at the bottom and royalty at the top — began to break down bit by bit. Because people were looking back and reimagining something older, this period is considered a "rebirth," rather than a completely new way of looking at the world. Leonardo was born at the perfect time to make a lasting impact on the world. If he had been born a century earlier, he might have been condemned a heretic for his ideas and practices. If he had been born a century later, some of what he did might not have seemed as ground-breaking.

MAKING MONEY THE FLORENTINE WAY

The history of Florence immediately following the birth of Leonardo was not all blood and battle. In fact, when the da Vinci family entered the historical record, the city of Florence was riding a wave of financial success. Despite all the fighting and bloody internal struggles, the Florentines were never known as warriors. They knew how to fight, certainly, but their real passion — and the source of their power — lay in their abilities as merchants and bankers.

---

7. "Signoria: Italian Medieval Government." *Encyclopedia Britannica*. 20 July 1998. Web. 20 Feb. 2017.

By the time of Leonardo's great-great-grandfather, Ser Guido, Florence had established itself as a major industrial and commercial power in all of Europe. Although not a port city like Venice, Florence still had easy access to the sea and quickly developed commercial connections the world over. Its products — most famously wool and other cloth — were sold in the Middle East, Africa, and England. The stability of their economy allowed the Florentines to create a type of money that soon became the most valued currency in the world: the gold florin. With a presence in every major town in Europe and the Middle East, the Florentines soon established themselves as leading businessmen. Their reputation also made them the preferred moneylenders in Europe.

Of course, this money wasn't available to every Florentine. Much of the wealth was concentrated in the same class that made up the Signoria — the merchants and nobles. In the time just before Leonardo, the major figures in the Florentine economy were the Bardi and the Peruzzi. These families had gathered so much wealth and power that they had business offices in places as far away as Jerusalem and Constantinople (modern-day Istanbul, Turkey). Their network of money connected them to the major powers of the day: the pope in Rome, the kings of England and France, and all the cities in Italy.

To add to their sense of power, many of these foreign rulers owed money to the Bardi and Peruzzi families. In the 1340's — the time that Ser Guido was actively working as a notary in Florence — King Edward III of England borrowed 600,000 gold Florins from the Peruzzi and 900,000 from the Bardi. Unfortunately for the Florentine bankers, they forgot that the English king saw himself as God's chosen ruler of the English people on earth. What are financial obligations to a man of such stature? When he was unable to pay back the Italian bankers, King Edward III simply ignored his debt. This promptly resulted in the collapse of the Bardi and Peruzzi banking houses.

The disaster of the two families was not enough to dampen the economy of Florence, and the wheels of commerce continued to spin. To take the place of the Bardi and the Peruzzi, two more families stepped in: the Pazzi and the Medici. It would be these two families, especially the Medici, that would play a major role in the life of Leonardo da Vinci.[8]

THE FOUNDATION OF LEONARDO'S WORLD

This, then, was the world that Leonardo was born into. It was a world of conflicting social classes, of internal and external struggles, and of wealthy and powerful people who were looking for ways to outdo each other. The threat of civil war within, and external battles without, was very real at all times. These power struggles, especially those between the different Italian cities and their larger neighbors outside, would define Leonardo's life. From the moment he entered the city of Florence, and as he grew as an artist, others determined the path of his life as much he did. He would be remembered as a genius of his time, and his time was one of change — of renaissance.

---

8. Goldthwaite, Richard A. *The Building of Renaissance Florence: An Economic and Social History*. Maryland: The Johns Hopkins UP, 1980. Print, 44-46.

CHAPTER 2

The Childhood of Leonardo

*L*eonardo entered this world of conflict and change at exactly 10:30 P.M. on Saturday, April 15th, 1452. We know these details thanks to his grandfather, Antonio, who was present in the small cottage. In a cramped hand, the 80-year-old Antonio noted down the event on the back page of a notebook that had belonged to *his* grandfather, Ser Guido.

> *"1452. There was born to me a grandson, the son of Ser Piero my son, on the 15th day of April, a Saturday, at the 3rd hour of the night. He bears the name Lionardo."*

In Renaissance Italy, time was determined by the number of hours before or after specific prayers given at monasteries. In this case, the last prayer happened at sunset. From this, we can determine that Leonardo was born around 10:30 P.M. Antonio continued his record keeping, noting that Leonardo was duly baptized by the parish priest who happened to be the family's next-door neighbor.

From church documents, we know that his baptism was a full-blown affair with 10 godparents stepping forward to represent the young babe at the ceremony. If the da Vinci family followed the custom of the day, Leonardo's baptism would have been followed by a big party, complete with tables full of food and jugs of wine made from the family's vineyards. Family and friends would have been invited, and even strangers from the neighborhood would eat a plate or two in celebration. A healthy baby boy christened and pledged to God was a joyous occasion!

By all accounts, Leonardo was fully welcomed into the da Vinci family. This is odd since he was illegitimate, a child born out of wedlock. As we already know, Leonardo's father came from a relatively established family. In addition to his notary business in the city of Florence, Ser Piero and the da Vinci family had land around Vinci and a house in what we would today describe as the suburbs of the small town. To the other townspeople, Ser Piero would have been a dignified man indeed, although not noble or excessively wealthy. He likely came from a higher social class than the woman who had borne him his son.

We know next to nothing about Caterina, Leonardo's mother. Some sources say she was a servant girl, possibly even in the service of the da Vinci family. Whether Ser Piero loved Caterina or not is now impossible to say, but within eight months of Leonardo's birth, Ser Piero married a rich Florentine notary's daughter named Albiera. At just 16 years old, Albiera was a young bride even for the times. It is likely that this marriage had been arranged years earlier before Ser Piero had even met Albiera or Leonardo's mother, Caterina. The idea behind the marriage would have been one of practicality: Ser Piero would gain social status and possible wealth by marrying a woman attached to an important business contact. Perhaps this arrangement is why he discarded Caterina so soon after Leonardo's birth. Whatever the reason, Caterina herself married a man of low-birth shortly thereafter.

Therefore, at the age of about one, Leonardo had a fractured life. Split between his father and stepmother and his mother and stepfather, Leonardo's childhood would have been one of complicated relationships.[9]

---

9. Nicholl, Charles. *Leonardo Da Vinci: Flights of the Mind*. New York, NY: Penguin, 2005. Print, 23-25.

When Caterina married Leonardo's stepfather (a man named Accatabriga), she went to live with him on a small farm near Campo Zeppi. Historians argue whether Leonardo went with his mother to Campo Zeppi or whether he was given to his grandfather Antonio and his wife to raise.[10] It is possible that Caterina took the infant Leonardo with her for at least a few years. After all, Campo Zeppi was located on hills overlooking the town of Vinci and just a short walk from the da Vinci land. It would have been more convenient for Caterina to raise her son than the 80-year-old Antonio and his 60-year-old wife.

Whatever the case, Leonardo would have remained in some contact with his mother while she was living with her new husband. Caterina and Accatabriga's first child together came when Leonardo was just two or three years old, and several more followed. Within a few years, the Accatabriga household would have been full of their children — and we wonder where Leonardo would have fit in.

Fun Fact

Accatabriga was a nickname and literally means "troublemaker" in Italian. Accatabriga's real name was Antonio di Piero Buti del Vacca, but he was always known first as Accatabriga. Usually, that nickname was given to soldiers or others who led a life of conflict, so it probably does give us an idea of the character of the man.

Whatever the particulars of his early childhood, whether living with Caterina and Accatabriga or with his grandparents, Leonardo most likely had little contact with his father. Ser Piero spent most of his time in Florence

---

10. Bramly, Serge. *Leonardo: The Artist and the Man*. London: Penguin, 1994. Print, 42-43.

with his young wife, Albiera. Unlike his mother, Leonardo's father and stepmother struggled to have children. In fact, his father played such a minor role in his upbringing that Leonardo's earliest biographer mistakenly said that Ser Piero was Leonardo's uncle instead of father.[11] We can only imagine how Leonardo felt, tossed between families while his mother and father went on with separate lives.

It is little wonder that Leonardo soon found himself very close to the only two people who appeared as role models to his young eyes: his grandfather Antonio and his uncle Francesco. Francesco and his father, Antonio, were cut from the same cloth. Both men retreated from the cosmopolitan Florence in favor of a settled country life in Vinci. While his brother, Ser Piero, pursued business and influential connections his whole life, Francesco remained on the family's property and managed the farms and estate. In a 1498 tax record, Francesco admits, "I am in the country without prospect of employment." Of course, no employment did not mean Francesco was poor. Like his father Antonio, Francesco lived on the money made from the family farms, which produced wheat, millet, wine, and olives for making oil. At just 15 when Leonardo was born, Francesco was like an older brother to the young artist and would be extremely close to his nephew for most of his life.[12]

This, then, was Leonardo's family. Neither completely a part of the da Vinci household nor that of his mother and stepfather, Leonardo was lost somewhere in between. We will never know the psychological impact this fractured family life had on the man, but it certainly played a part in creating the artist we now know.

---

11. Vasari, Giorgio. *The Lives of the Artists*. Trans. Julia C. Bondanella and Peter Bondanella. New York: Oxford UP, 1991. Print, 558-559.
12. Nicholl, Charles. *Leonardo Da Vinci: Flights of the Mind*. New York, NY: Penguin, 2005. Print., 25.

GROWING UP IN AND AROUND VINCI

Just as important in forming the character of Leonardo were the fields he played in and the animals he saw. Nature, for Leonardo, would be a life-long love affair. The rolling Tuscan hills surrounding Vinci and other rural scenes from his childhood would reappear as the backdrop in his paintings and as doodles in the margins of his journals.

Fun Fact

The word Vincio — which inspired the name of Vinci and, therefore, Leonardo's family name — is an old Italian word that means osier. An osier is a species of willow plant that grows along the river banks in northern Italy. The roots of these willows were harvested by the locals and woven into baskets. The town of Vinci during Leonardo's time was known for these beautiful baskets. Leonardo's expertise at drawing braided hair and other intricate patterns may be because, as a boy, he saw elders weaving osier roots.

Then, as now, Northern Italy had relatively mild weather. It was sticky-hot in the summer but cool and wet in the winter — with some snowfall in the higher elevations. The town of Vinci itself was built near the banks of the Vincio River and surrounded by gentle hills of olive orchards, vineyards, and other agricultural crops.

Leonardo grew up on a farm, whether that of his mother and stepfather at Campo Zeppi or his grandparents nearer to Vinci. Besides not having tractors and other machines to make the work easier, farm life in Renaissance Italy wouldn't have been that much different from farm life today. Leonardo would have accompanied his uncle Francesco as the older man surveyed the family's holdings around the town, checking in on farmers who

rented the land from the da Vinci.[13] These formal business outings probably didn't suit the antsy young Leonardo, who even as a child would have
preferred the independent life he would eventually lead as an artist.

It isn't an exaggeration to say that most of Leonardo's childhood was spent
outdoors, splashing in the Vincio River, dashing along the dirt cart paths
that stretched along the landscape, and lying back in a bed of poppy flow-
ers watching the puffy clouds waft by. Perhaps nature served as an escape
for the young boy. After all, the fields don't care who runs through them,
the gentle breeze ruffles the hair of the noble- and illegitimate-born alike.
There in the wild, Leonardo could be free from the cares of his world.
Rather than eventually fading into the background as familiar things often
do, nature constantly amazed and intrigued Leonardo for the rest of his
life. Each rock, bush, and streambed provided fresh insight. Nature would
be an important obsession of his life, and the landscape of the Italian countryside would remain dear to his heart.

Related to his love and fascination of nature was his equal love of animals —
a passion that certainly started when he was a boy on the farm. Then, as
now, a farm was not complete without a whole collection of animals. Sheep,
hogs, horses, dogs, and cats would call the countryside home — and these
were just the domesticated animals! The woods would have been filled with
foxes, rabbits, and deer and the sky with birds of all different feathers.
Leonardo grew up surrounded by life, an awareness that might have been
the cause for his eventually becoming a vegetarian later in life. In an age
when meat was quite expensive and often only available to the well-to-do,
everyone wanted some. It was strange, therefore, for a man to steer clear of
the stuff.

---

13. Bramly, Serge. *Leonardo: The Artist and the Man.* London: Penguin, 1994. Print, 45.

Fun Fact

Most of what we know about Leonardo's life and work comes from the man himself in the form of personal journals he kept. We should think of these journals less as diaries and more as his personal documents. Written on varying sizes of often loose-leaf paper, they give us a glimpse into the mind of the master. Today, over 7,000 pages of these journals survive in museum collections around the world, and we know he wrote many thousands more in his lifetime that have since disappeared. Sometimes, the pages are crowded with weird cartoonish doodles that he scratched out of boredom or entertainment. Other times, the pages contain paragraphs written by Leonardo on a wide range of topics: human anatomy, natural history, philosophy, and art. These pages also contain artistic studies of human posture, plants waving in the wind, and countless other everyday things that intrigued him enough to draw. Without a doubt, if we did not have these manuscripts, we would know next to nothing about Leonardo da Vinci, and the world would have been poorer because of it.

It was certainly here on the farm as a child that Leonardo first learned to ride a horse. Later in life, he was known as a connoisseur of horses, although this might have only been by the standards of the city slickers of Florence.[14] Leonardo's journals that have survived the centuries are full of drawings of animals. Although he drew some of these pictures as studies (drawings made as practice to learn how to capture the gesture or look of something), this wasn't always the case. Some animals, like one particular female cat, appear so frequently that we might be tempted to think that Leonardo was drawing his pets![15]

---

14. Vasari, Giorgio. *The Lives of the Artists*. Trans. Julia C. Bondanella and Peter Bondanella. New York: Oxford UP, 1991. Print, 286.
15. Nicholl, Charles. *Leonardo Da Vinci: Flights of the Mind*. New York, NY: Penguin, 2005. Print., 43.

Don't Just Take my Word for It!

Leonardo's earliest biographer, Giorgio Vasari, tells us, "When passing by places where birds were being sold, [Leonardo] would often take them out of their cages with his own hands, and after paying the seller the price that was asked of him, he would set them free in the air, restoring to them the liberty they had lost."[16]

If Leonardo made friends as a child, he never wrote about them. But rare is the child who doesn't pal around with someone, even if it was only to get into a little trouble! When he was an adult working and living in Florence, Leonardo surrounded himself with young men who enjoyed a good practical joke or two, sometimes done at the expense of Leonardo himself. We can imagine then that as a boy he found a similar group of hooligans to pass the time with and probably cause some headaches to the local farmers.[17]

LEONARDO: THE BUDDING ARTIST

If the picture we have painted of Leonardo's childhood is one of a quaint country life, that's because it probably was one. However, his youth wasn't entirely spent frolicking in nature and getting into trouble with friends. After all, as anyone who has lived on a farm knows, there is a never-ending list of things to do.

---

16. Vasari, Giorgio. The Lives of the Artists. Trans. Julia C. Bondanella and Peter Bondanella. New York: Oxford UP, 1991. Print, 286.
17. Bramly, Serge. Leonardo: The Artist and the Man. London: Penguin, 1994. Print, 113.

Fun Fact

Although today we think of Italian as a single language, during Leonardo's life there were many different dialects (or types) of spoken Italian. Some of these dialects were so different from the others that two people meeting might not be able to understand each other even though they both lived in what we now call Italy!

Living as he was with either his mother and stepfather, or his grandparents and uncle, Leonardo would have quickly been put to work cleaning the house, hauling water from the well to the animals, and generally being of service to the adults in his life. Between chores at home, walking around the countryside, and just being an ordinary kid, we have to wonder when Leonardo had time to prepare for becoming the preeminent artist of his age. Artistic geniuses don't just sprout up overnight. Surely, Leonardo was trained from birth for the art world?

Well, actually, he wasn't. In fact, historians today are certain that up until Leonardo travelled to Florence as a young teenager to apprentice as an artist, he had very little education in art. An even more surprising fact is that he didn't have much of an education at all. When he was an adult writing in his journal, Leonardo remarked that he was "an unlettered man." By that he didn't mean he was illiterate (after all he was *writing* in the journal). Rather, by "unlettered" he meant that he couldn't read and write in the language of the educated. You see, in Renaissance Italy — and for centuries before and after — all those who were educated could read and write in Latin, the language of the ancient Romans. All over the western world, most of the legal and official proceedings were written in Latin. In fact, the Latin language was the international language of the Medieval and Renaissance world. Whether you were French, Spanish, or Italian, if you were a member of a certain social class and had the education, you all had one thing in common: Latin.

However, this wasn't the case for illegitimate sons of mid-level notaries in small country towns. That's not to say that Leonardo had no education whatsoever. After all, even though he was illegitimate, he was a da Vinci! His father Ser Piero would have seen that his son received some basic schooling, probably from his local parish priest. Leonardo would have been taught to read and write in the local dialect of Vinci. This was his mother tongue, and when he eventually did go to Florence to live, he probably spoke with a "country" accent quite distinct from the accent spoken in the city. Writing later in life, Leonardo remarked that "I have so many words in my mother tongue that I should rather complain of not understanding things well than of lacking words with which to express the ideas in my head."[18] So, as you can see, he certainly was quite the "lettered" man, he just didn't know the type of letters that mattered!

Fun Fact

It was probably because of his lack of a formal education that Leonardo wrote in a "mirror script." Take a look at one of his notebooks and you'll see that not only did he write from right to left, but his very letters were backwards (his "d" looked like "b" and so on). Later scholars would say that this strange writing style was used as a sort of code, devised by the great thinker to keep people from reading his work and stealing his ideas. More likely, it was simply because he was left-handed and didn't want to smudge his writing by dragging his hand across it (try writing left-handed yourself and you'll see what I mean!). If Leonardo had gone to a formal school, his teachers probably would have trained the young boy to write right-handed instead.

---

18. Nicholl, Charles. *Leonardo Da Vinci: Flights of the Mind*. New York, NY: Penguin, 2005. Print., 54.

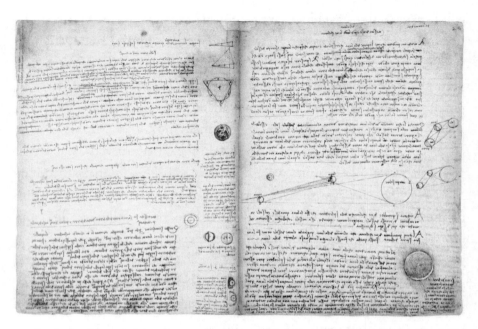

Example of Leonardo's mirror script from notebook pages with the letters facing backwards and the script flowing from right to left — {{PD-1923}}

In addition to his lack of formal education, Leonardo probably had no training in art before moving to Florence. Today, we are exposed to thousands of images every time we walk out of our houses. From advertisements on billboards, buses, and newspapers to commercials on the internet and TV, we live in a very visual world. That wasn't the case in 15th-century Italy. The only images that Leonardo would have been exposed to growing up in Vinci would have been paintings found in local churches. These religious scenes of Christ's crucifixion or the Virgin Mary holding the infant Jesus were all the more moving to believers because no other images existed to compete for their attention. For a budding artist like Leonardo, each Sunday would have been an exhilarating opportunity to soak in artwork.

So, what sort of art was there in the local church of Vinci? Not much. In fact, the only piece that we know was present in the church of Santa Croce where Leonardo was baptized and attended weekly mass is a painted wood sculpture of Mary Magdalene. While not made by a renowned artist of the period, the sculpture was certainly executed by a pupil of one, perhaps a student of the great Donatello. Beyond the borders of Vinci, there were more pieces of Renaissance art that the young Leonardo might have admired, but no one knows for certain if he ever visited these cities as a child.[19] It is also possible that his grandfather Antonio had in his home a few pieces, like a painted crucifix or a brightly painted, carved wood chest. However, while the da Vinci were relatively well-off, in Renaissance Italy art was for the elite or wealthy.[20] Therefore, the boy who would grow into the greatest artist of his generation received no artistic training and very little exposure to it while growing up at home.

Leonardo's childhood would have been a mixed bag. Born the illegitimate son of a middleclass family, he would have been caught between the woman who gave birth to him and the man who gave him his last name. Raised by an odd collection of people — his stepfather, mother, grandparents, uncle, father, and stepmother — Leonardo would learn at an early age to deal with uncertainties. Life is full of them, and the sooner you learn to be flexible, the better you will be at surviving. This would be the mantra of Leonardo's life. Despite the challenges of his birth, he lived a relatively comfortable childhood. Growing up on a farm, he would have taken the chores and work in stride, enjoying the fun romps over the countryside when he could. If he couldn't always look to his mother or father for support, there was always his uncle Francesco. Things could be worse for young Leonardo.

---

19. Ibid. 56-57.
20. Bramly, Serge. *Leonardo: The Artist and the Man*. London: Penguin, 1994. Print, 60.

CHAPTER 3

Leonardo the Apprentice

Childhoods, even the happiest, don't last forever. Leonardo's ended abruptly when he arrived in Florence in the back of that rickety cart in 1466. The journey that had taken the young teenager from Vinci to the big city of Florence wasn't completely foreign to him. After all, his father did live primarily in the city and as a boy Leonardo probably visited him — even if it was only rarely. But this trip was different. Leonardo was coming to live in Florence for good.

In 1466, Leonardo was just 14 years old — a country kid who had spent most of his life among the hills and fields of Vinci. He was most at home walking barefoot along the dusty country paths that wandered around the rural landscape, not shod in boots dodging crowds of people in one of Florence's many plazas. But the young boy had no say in the matter. Like many points in his life, Leonardo was washed along by the roaring stream of circumstances outside of his control.

How the illegitimate son of a mid-level notary even found himself an apprentice to an artist in Florence isn't known for certain. We know that he had few opportunities during his childhood to even see great art, so how on earth did he develop sufficient talent to even be recognized as a potential artist? And who was the first person to discover this ability hidden inside the quiet young boy?

Don't Just Take my Word for It!

The Florence that Leonardo entered was a growing city. A visitor in the mid-1400s noted the sheer size of the place. In his account, we learn that the walls surrounding the city stretched seven miles and were fortified with 80 watchtowers. Within the walls, 108 churches provided places for worship and 50 plazas offered space for people to build markets and congregate. There were also 33 banks, 270 woolworker's shops, and 83 silkworker's shops that specialized in making the fine clothing Florence was known for.[21]

The answer to the first question is lost in the shadows of time. Like most geniuses, Leonardo was probably born with some innate artistic talent that forced its way to the surface despite his rural surroundings. The answer to the second question is clearer. Ironically, it appears that the person who had the least contact with the boy during his childhood was the one responsible for his discovery. Ser Piero, Leonardo's absentee father, had become a relatively successful notary during the time his young son was growing up in Vinci. Recently, he had done some work for monasteries and convents in and around Florence. During the Renaissance, places of religious worship and contemplation commissioned some of the most spectacular art of the day. Alongside the wealthy elite of cities, these religious orders were the financial force behind artists like Leonardo da Vinci.

While writing contracts and otherwise providing legal services, Ser Piero would have met some of the artists these places were hiring. Perhaps it was during one of his everyday visits to a client that Ser Piero bumped into the artist Andrea Verrocchio. A very well-regarded artist of his time, Andrea operated an artist studio in Florence.[22]

---

21. Fanelli, Giovanni. *Brunelleschi*. Firenze: Scala, 1980. Print 82-85.
22. Bramly, Serge. *Leonardo: The Artist and the Man*. London: Penguin, 1994. Print, 62.

We can imagine the scene ourselves: Ser Piero and Andrea making small-talk, and Ser Piero producing a small drawing his young son made for him and showing it to the artist. "Does my son have potential?" he might have asked. Andrea, looking at the drawing, might have seen some small kernel of the boy's true genius. Andrea agreed to take on Leonardo as an apprentice and train him in the ways of a Renaissance artist. Back in Vinci for a brief break from the city, Ser Piero would have informed Leonardo that he had secured the boy a good future. The deal was struck and, just like that, Leonardo's fate flowed along the torrential stream of chance towards Florence and a new world.

CULTURE SHOCK

Coughing in the cloud of dust kicked up by the retreating horse-drawn cart, the 14-year-old Leonardo would have stood silently in front of the stone-faced house. Inside, his father was awaiting him, ready to get him moved into Andrea's studio as soon as possible. After all, the boy's future wasn't in the world of notaries. As an illegitimate child, Leonardo legally couldn't work in the family trade — which was just one more harsh reality he'd have to face in life.

Ser Piero had recently moved to this prestigious house on the Via della Prestanze after he married his second wife, Francesca. Albiera, Ser Piero's first wife, had died in 1464 while giving birth to what was going to be his first legitimate child. Unfortunately, both mother and baby died and Ser Piero, almost 40 years old, was once more without wife or legitimate heir. He wasn't long a widower, however. Making yet another advantageous move, Ser Piero looked to "marry up" in the world. He found Francesca, the 15-year-old daughter of one of his business contacts. Shortly after the introductions were made, the two were wed.

Soon after the death of Albiera, Ser Piero's own aged father, Antonio, had also died. The loss of his grandfather must have been quite a blow to the young Leonardo, made even worse by his uncle leaving the house and marrying a woman himself. In just two short years, Leonardo had lost a stepmother and grandfather to death and a dear uncle to a new bride. It would have been with an emptiness and sadness that Leonardo regarded the front door to his father's home.

We don't know how Francesca, just one year older than Leonardo himself, regarded her new husband's illegitimate child. Strangely enough, Ser Piero's first wife had bonded with Leonardo over the years before her death. The two were close enough that Leonardo would remain in contact with her brother for many years to come.[23] The same relationship probably did not blossom between Francesca and Leonardo. After all, there wouldn't have been much time for it. Leonardo was bound for the studio of Andrea Verrocchio. There, he would spend the next 11 years of his life.

LEARNING THE ROPES

By the time Leonardo entered Andrea's studio in 1466, Andrea was a well-recognized artist. Ser Piero had chosen well for his son, even if the young Leonardo wasn't willing to admit it himself right away. As an apprentice, Leonardo lived and worked in Andrea's studio alongside several other apprentices. In place of his grandparent's house in the countryside, Leonardo now found himself a part of a different kind of family. He, alongside the several other young apprentices, had become a part of Andrea's extended family. Andrea would feed him, house him, and educate him. We don't know how much Ser Piero paid Andrea for this privilege, but it was probably a considerable amount.

---

23. Nicholl, Charles. *Leonardo Da Vinci: Flights of the Mind*. New York, NY: Penguin, 2005. Print.61-62.

Fun Fact

It was quite common for Renaissance artists to take the last name of the master artists that they studied under. For instance, Andrea took the last name "Verrocchio" from his first master, Francesco di Luca Verrocchio. At the time, it was a mark of great distinction to be taught by a famous master artisan. And by taking a master's name, an apprentice could show the world that he knew his stuff. Think of it as a letter of recommendation, but one that stayed with you your whole life![24]

Andrea himself was an interesting character. Born Andrea di Michele di Francesco Cione, he was the son of a brick and tile maker. Just like Leonardo, he came from a middleclass family. Andrea's life nearly turned disastrous when, at the early age of 17, he almost threw it all away in one single foolish act. While hanging out with friends outside of the city walls one afternoon, he was throwing rocks around when one of them accidentally struck his companion in the head. The young Antonio di Domenico died several days after the incident, and Andrea was charged with his murder. Although the court acquitted the young man of the charges, Andrea never forgot his actions, and some say the melancholy aspect of his later artistic work reflects his deep-seated regrets.

It was probably around this time that Andrea entered the studio of one Francesco di Luca Verrocchio, a renowned goldsmith of Florence. For several years under Verrocchio, Andrea learned the art of molding, engraving, and working in gold — a craft that taught him an attention to detail that he would later use in all his other work. Andrea later learned under the famous artist Donatello, who taught the young goldsmith the art of sculpture. From

---

24. Burke, Peter. *The Italian Renaissance: Culture and Society in Italy.* Cambridge: Polity, 2014. Print, 56.

another master, he learned painting; and from yet another, engineering. By the time he set up his own studio, Andrea was a jack-of-all-trades.[25]

Don't Just Take my Word for It!

When Andrea died in 1488, an inventory was made of his studio. Take a look at some of the quirky contents of a Renaissance artist's workshop!

- 1 feather bed with white bed-cover, mattress, pair of sheets and painted bed frame

- 1 dining room table and bench

- 1 bucket for well

- 1 chest to keep grain in

- 1 jar of oil

- 3 casks containing 14 barrels of wine

- 1 large case of vinegar wine

- 1 model of a building

25. Cruttwell, Maud. *Verrocchio*. New York: Charles Scribner's Sons, 1904. Print, 25-27.

- 1 fine lute (musical instrument)
- 1 Bible and a series of other books
- 1 picture of the head of Andrea (a portrait)
- 1 terracotta sculpture of a baby
- 1 large painting
- 1 kiln with various iron tools
- 5 molds for making cannon balls[26]

In studios like Andrea's, there was endless diversity of projects. Over the years, his studio produced paintings in various sizes, from large murals to small devotionals; sculptures in marble, bronze, and wood; gold and silver work; tombstones; carved and painted wood marriage chests; jousting pennants, banners, and costumes for parades; and so much more. Andrea's studio was basically a commercial factory of high end products.

The studio itself was located in the district of Sant'Ambrogio within the city — just a short walk from Ser Piero's own notary office. If Andrea's was like other typical artist studios, it would have consisted of a large open room or courtyard on the ground floor that opened to the street. The apprentices would share rooms behind this central space, and the master would live upstairs.

With projects ranging from woodworking, goldsmithing, and painting, a constant cacophony of sounds and smells would assault anyone entering the workshop from the street. The acrid stench of varnish for the wood and paints, the hammering of iron, and the roar of the forge — this was the

---

26. Nicholl, Charles. *Leonardo Da Vinci: Flights of the Mind.* New York, NY: Penguin, 2005. Print, 76.

world Leonardo entered in 1466. He obviously found something to his liking — he never turned back.[27]

The duties given to new apprentices were tedious, but each one of them was meant to teach the pupil some aspect of his future trade. With such a variety of projects in the works, Leonardo was kept constantly busy in Andrea's studio. In the early years of his apprenticeship, he focused on small aspects of the trade. Painting in Renaissance Italy required a great deal of preparation, and it was up to the apprentices to learn these mechanics of art before they could actually put paintbrush to wood panel.

When we think of paintings today, we think of pictures painted onto linen canvas or maybe paper. In Renaissance Italy, however, many of the paintings were painted onto wood panels. White poplar was the preferred wood, but you couldn't just take any old panel and start painting a masterpiece on it! It took quite a bit of preparation beforehand. For Leonardo and the other apprentices, learning how to prepare these wood panels was one of the first steps in their education. First, once the panel was chosen and cut to size, the apprentice applied a base layer of white paint. Each artist had his own recipe for making the perfect basecoat of paint (also known as gesso). A generic gesso would consist of white chalk, gypsum (a type of mineral), water, and an animal-based glue substance to hold everything together on the panel.[28]

Later in life, Leonardo would reveal the recipe for his own custom-made gesso:

> *"Coat [the panel] over with mastic and white turpentine twice distilled . . . then give it two or three coats of aqua vitae in which you*

27. Ibid 73.
28. Ibid. 82.

have dissolved arsenic, or some other corrosive sublimate two or three times. Then apply boiled linseed oil in such a way that it may penetrate every part, and before it is cold rub it well with a cloth to dry it. Over this apply a liquid white varnish with a stick, then wash it with urine."[29]

Did you get all of that? Yeah, me neither, but Leonardo swore by it. Arsenic, linseed oil, and urine — not the most pleasant of substances. Mixing the pre-measured amounts of this stuff and prepping the panels with it would have been the apprentice Leonardo's job in the studio. Between learning the mechanics of art and doing general house cleaning and running errands, Leonardo and the other apprentices were kept busy under Andrea's care.

FINALLY! LEARNING TO PAINT — ALMOST

Each one of these unglamorous tasks was integral to the functioning of the studio. Of course, the apprentices were also there to learn how to draw, capture the essences of an image, and reproduce it on a wood panel. But that took time. Nothing happened quickly in the training of a Renaissance artist. Leonardo himself, when he operated his own studio, would not allow young apprentices under the age of 20 to even touch brushes or colors, forcing them instead to practice with lead or silver-pointed styluses.[30] A metal point stylus, sometimes made of lead but also occasionally silver, acted similarly to our modern-day graphite pencils.

Because paper was expensive in Renaissance Italy, apprentices likely practiced their drawing on wood panels coated in white ash or another type of

29. Leonardo. *The Notebooks of Leonardo Da Vinci, Complete.* Trans. Jean Paul Richter. Dover Publications, Inc., 1972. Electronic. 280.
30. Pedretti, Carlo. *The Literary Works of Leonardo da Vinci, Compiled and Edited from the Original Manuscripts by Jean Paul Richter.* Oxford: Phaidon, 1977, vol. 1. Print, 11.

light material that could adhere to the wood. In the early years of Leonardo's training, this is likely what he spent many hours doing. Andrea would place a clay model of a young man's head on a chair facing his pupils and tell them to draw the head on their wood panels. Then he would turn the model to the side and the apprentices would practice a side view. Gradually, Andrea would up the ante, challenging his young pupils to learn more difficult techniques.

Fun Fact

Leonardo would have also spent a great deal of time simply copying drawings made by Andrea himself. By his apprentices copying them as part of their training in art, they themselves inevitably absorbed some of the techniques of their master. This is how art historians can identify the particular master, or "school," that a Renaissance artist taught under. Hidden deep within each artist's later work are small details that lead back to their teacher's influence. Leonardo's early works definitely contain echoes of his tutor, Andrea Verrocchio.[31]

As an apprentice, Leonardo learned how to realistically draw the folds of clothing on a person's body by draping actual linen sheets on clay models and spending hours on end scrapping his silver-pointed stylus against the wood panel and shading in the shadows with black ink. This meticulous practice stayed with Leonardo his entire life and filled the thousands of pages of his journal with what appear to be random images of people's hands, legs, heads, and clothes.

31. Burke, Peter. *The Italian Renaissance: Culture and Society in Italy.* Cambridge: Polity, 2014. Print, 58.

Eventually, Andrea allowed Leonardo and the rest of the apprentices to practice with live models of people and animals. Sometimes the apprentices themselves posed as models for the others or for Andrea as inspiration for an actual commissioned piece. Later in life, Leonardo would take this modelling one step further and dissect dead animals and people to learn how their muscles and ligaments worked — all the better to depict them realistically in his paintings.

Don't Just Take my Word for It!

Leonardo writes,

"The youth should first learn perspective, then the proportions of objects. Then he may copy some good master, to accustom himself to fine forms. Then from nature to confirm by practice the rules he has learnt. Then see for a time the works of various masters. Then get the habit of putting his art into practice and work."[32]

ANDREA'S STUDIO: THE PLACE TO BE

And so, Leonardo was thrown headfirst into a completely new world, forced to either swim or drown. To the cosmopolitan Florentines, Leonardo seemed a country bumpkin. His deep tanned body and scraggly curly hair marked him as out-of-place even before he could open his mouth to speak — which was just as well, because Leonardo spoke in a thick Vinci accent. Kids can be extremely cruel, and we can only imagine how Leonardo would have been picked on for being different. His first few years in Andrea's studio were likely difficult ones.

---

32. Leonardo. *The Notebooks of Leonardo Da Vinci, Complete*. Trans. Jean Paul Richter. Dover Publications, Inc., 1972. Electronic. 212.

Eventually, though, Leonardo carved out a niche for himself. Each one of them vying for the attention and approval of their master, Leonardo and his fellow apprentices certainly had their quarrels. History, however, did not record any, and what we are left with is a picture of a leading artist studio that trained some of the most talented youth of the day.

Andrea's studio proved more than that, though. His workshop was quickly becoming the meeting place for the new wave of Renaissance art, making it the perfect place for Leonardo to be. Beyond his fellow apprentices, Leonardo met some of the premiere artists of his day during his time with Andrea. Artists who either learned techniques from Andrea or the other way around, these shining stars in the art scene of Florence orbited around Andrea's studio. The young Leonardo became familiar with the likes of Pietro Perugino and Sandro Botticelli.[33] If you don't know these men, it is only because Leonardo has since become so renowned that he's overshadowed their work.

For the years he was studying under Andrea, however, Leonardo was just one of several promising young artists in a studio full of them. In fact, it was not Leonardo who became the teacher's pet, but a younger apprentice by the name of Lorenzo di Credi. Lorenzo would eventually take over Andrea's studio and was made his heir when the great teacher died.[34]

When Leonardo came to Florence in 1466, he was unanchored from the world. He had recently lost his grandfather, a man who had more to do with his upbringing than his own father, as well as his stepmother. Still stinging from his uncle Francesco leaving him, Leonardo must have felt alone in the world. He found his place among the hustle and bustle of an

---

33. Bramly, Serge. *Leonardo: The Artist and the Man.* London: Penguin, 1994. Print, 73.
34. Nicholl, Charles. *Leonardo Da Vinci: Flights of the Mind.* New York, NY: Penguin, 2005. Print, 87.

artist studio. Although not the favorite pupil in the studio, Leonardo quickly proved Andrea's hunch about him right: the boy had hidden talent. Years of hard work, study, and exposure to talented artists nourished that seed of genius. And soon, before he had even finished his apprenticeship, that seed grew and blossomed into the greatest artist of the Renaissance.

CHAPTER 4

A Youth in Florence

*S*itting on the hillside, his long legs sprawled in front of him towards the valley below, Leonardo da Vinci squinted against the noonday sun. It was summer 1473, and the 21-year-old Leonardo was enjoying a brief vacation from the stifling confines of Florence. On his lap sat a large piece of paper with the image of the landscape before him sketched into the soft surface. The scene was certainly one worth drawing: small groves of trees broke the monotony of the grassy hillsides that rose abruptly out of the lush valley floor, and the terracotta rooftops of a small, walled town that looked insignificant among the rolls of endless farmland that disappeared into the distance. One last touch finished the drawing: "August 5, 1473."

Leonardo must have felt especially proud of his drawing, because at the time it was rare for artists to date their paintings — let alone a sketch. But, then again, Leonardo had plenty to be happy about that summer day in 1473. For the past seven years, he had settled into life in Florence, not only surviving in the bustling town, but thriving. The awkward, sunburnt country bumpkin of a boy had grown into a handsome young man. His curly hair fell in neat locks to his shoulders, and the beginnings of a beard shadowed the edges of his chin. Always one to stay on top of fashion trends, and preferring the neat and tidy over the dirty and unkempt, Leonardo as a young man appeared a different person entirely from the boy who had first walked into Andrea's workshop all those years ago.[35]

Leonardo had joined Andrea's studio at the perfect time. Beginning in the late 1460s, Andrea increasingly became the go-to artist for commissions — even taking requests from the city's leaders.

THE MEDICI: A FLORENTINE POWERHOUSE

When we talk about the "leaders" of Florence in the late 1460s, we mean just one family: the Medici. The Medici rose to prominence following the collapse of the banking families of the Peruzzi and Bardi in the middle 1300s. Taking advantage of this opening in the competition, the Medici bank increased its reach from Florence to Rome and beyond to Europe. By the time Leonardo's grandfather, Antonio, was enjoying life on his farm in the early 1400s, the Medici were securing their power in the city. At the head of the family was Cosimo de'Medici. Through the family's financial ties and his own political maneuvering, Cosimo secured his place at the head of Florence.

Although still a "republic" in name, by the time Leonardo was born, this one family essentially controlled the city. When Leonardo started his apprenticeship in 1466, Cosimo's son was in power, the great leader himself having since died. Nicknamed Piero "the Gouty" because he suffered from gout, Piero differed a lot from his late father. Whereas Cosimo was raised a banker and could talk with a cobbler on the streets just as easily as with the Pope in Rome, Piero was raised like a prince. He came across as arrogant and entitled and failed at playing the role of the "politician of the people,"

---

35. Kemp, Martin. *Leonardo*. Oxford: Oxford UP, 2011. Print, 43-46.

which was an important ruse because the Medici's position in Florence was not technically legal under a republic. [36]

LEONARDO'S FIRST ENCOUNTER

In 1469, as Piero was suffering from an especially painful inflammation of gout, his own son Lorenzo decided to throw a citywide celebration. Lorenzo de'Medici, nicknamed "il Magnifico" (the Magnificent), was a spectacular politician and the polar opposite of his father. He would need all that skill to keep the reins of power firmly within the grasp of the Medici during the rocky reign of Piero. Not only was Piero a less-than-popular ruler, but the plague was once again making its way through Italian cities and killing thousands. The wave of the plague crashed against the walls of Florence just as Leonardo had begun to settle into life in the studio, providing the teenager his first experience with the disease. It wouldn't be his last.

Fun Fact

The word "Medici" in Italian means doctor, and it might be a clue that in early Medieval Florence the Medici family practiced medicine before banking. The double meaning of the word causes some confusion for historians. For instance, when Leonardo wrote later in life "*Li medici mi crearono e distrussono,*" does he mean "Doctors created me and destroyed me" or "The Medici created me and destroyed me"? Was Leonardo an old man complaining about ill-health or about politics?[37]

36. Bartlett, Kenneth R. *A Short History of the Italian Renaissance*. Toronto: Toronto UP, 2013, Print, 107-108.
37. Nicholl, Charles. *Leonardo Da Vinci: Flights of the Mind*. New York, NY: Penguin, 2005. Print, 167.

Lorenzo hoped that the celebration would not only distract the citizens from the plague but also reaffirm the power of the Medici. On the surface, the festival was dedicated to a beautiful and very popular young woman in Florence, a certain Lucrezia Donati. Lorenzo was generous, and Medici money paid for most of the celebrations.

The festival itself took the form of a jousting tournament and parade. All the major families of the city sought the services of artists like Andrea Verrocchio to design and build their costumes. From Andrea's workshop, Lorenzo de'Medici himself ordered a large banner, as well as a painted portrait of the beautiful Lucrezia.

Lorenzo gave extremely specific instructions on what he was looking for in the banner — after all, appearances were everything. He ordered that the image of a sun and rainbow be woven onto the face and stitched into the fabric above should be the motto, "The time has returned." Placed somewhere amid this scene should also be a female figure weaving a garland of laurel leaves. At just 16 and a second-year apprentice, Leonardo assisted his master in creating both works. True to form, they crafted a masterpiece.

When Lorenzo beheld the banner, joy overtook him. And so began a long relationship between the Medici family and Andrea Verrocchio's studio.[38] It was a good thing that Andrea had made a good impression, because for the next several years the Medici would be busy with public projects that required the ability of a world-class artist and his studio. Following the celebration of Lucrezia Donati in February of 1469, public festivities were held again later that year when Lorenzo married a well-to-do young woman, Clarice Orsini. Andrea's studio certainly had commissions from this celebration as well, and Leonardo's education continued.

---

38. Bramly, Serge. *Leonardo: The Artist and the Man*. London: Penguin, 1994. Print, 91.

We can only imagine what Florence would have been like on festival days — banners and pennants hanging from windows as spectators crowded balconies and the sides of streets to catch sight of the parade of pageantry winding throughout the city; people dressed in fantastic costumes and wearing grotesque and fanciful masks capering down the streets, pounding drums, and tooting trumpets; food vendors hawking their wares; jugglers and acrobats cartwheeling among the crowd; and torches burning deep into the night until the sun of the new dawn lightened the sky. Florence in celebration would have been something to see! The noise, the smells, and the sheer thrill of the party would be enough to pull anyone into its stream — especially a young artist's apprentice like Leonardo.[39] Leonardo's life in Florence certainly wasn't all work.

Don't Just Take my Word for It!

Angelo Poliziano, a poet of the day, once said that all Florentines led a life of "blithe [indifferent] enjoyment." It may be an exaggeration, but Poliziano wasn't far off the mark. After all, between the dozens of religious festivals, visits from foreign dignitaries, and the marriages and birthdays of important people, there would have been a celebration in the city every week of the year.[40]

These whirlwind festivities initiated the young country boy into the thrilling and sometimes overwhelming life of a Renaissance city. All the revelers would have known who paid for the party: the Medici. The sheer extravagance on display during these festivities made the point that the Medici were not only wealthy and powerful, but they cared about the city and its people. Just like major corporations today sponsor sports teams and the venues in which the teams play (and get to advertise their name on the

---

39. Ibid, 92.
40. Ibid 88.

buildings or jerseys in return), so did the Medici have their stamp on all these celebrations. Each time he worked on commissions for festivals and other public projects, the apprentice Leonardo therefore learned an important lesson about how life worked in Renaissance Italy and the role of art in that world.

Powerful men like the Medici, and important institutions like city guilds and the Catholic Church, acquired and maintained power by any means necessary. Pieces of art — from festival banners to buildings and everything in between — were just one of those means. What better way to show one's social status and convey a message of strength than through art, the only visual media present in the 1400s? These early commissions also showed Leonardo that to be successful in his industry, he had to look to the powerful and wealthy. Struggling to create relationships with powerful people — and not always succeeding — would remain a part of Leonardo's career until his death.[41]

POODLES, PORTRAITS, AND PROFESSIONAL CREDENTIALS

Yes, Leonardo da Vinci had a lot to be happy about that summer day of 1473. In the seven years under Andrea, he had learned the way of the world and the place of art and artists in the struggle for power in Renaissance Italy. But for all his education in these worldly matters, he had only just begun to actually paint.

As we already learned, it took years of practice before apprentices were allowed to even touch a paintbrush — let alone conduct an entire painting. Finally, after several years of learning the basics, Leonardo had the opportunity to put paintbrush to wood panel, but only for a portion of a painting.

---

41. Burke, Peter. *The Italian Renaissance: Culture and Society in Italy*. Cambridge: Polity, 2014. Print, 138-148.

You see, most major paintings of the Renaissance period were group projects. The master artist would lay the scene out, deciding what figures went where and maybe even penciling them onto the wood panel. For some of the simpler features, like the background or sky, however, the artist would have his more experienced apprentices take over. So, the earliest known artistic endeavors of the young Leonardo aren't major paintings at all, but small parts of larger ones done by Andrea. It has taken centuries of close inspection for art historians to generally agree which paintings the apprentice Leonardo helped with — and even after all these years, we aren't completely sure!

Fun Fact

Those who commissioned works of art from studios knew that the masters liked to have their apprentices do some of the work. But when you pay for an artist to paint something for you, you definitely want to make sure you're getting your money's worth! That's why contracts between artists and patrons sometimes specified how much of the work could be done by an apprentice and how much had to be done by the master himself. If you wanted a work of art done 100 percent by the master, you had to be prepared to spend more money!

By comparing them to some of his later techniques, we think Leonardo painted the small poodle-like dog that runs yapping at the heels of the angel as well as the fish in Andrea's *Tobias and the Angel*. A childhood spent wild among the hills and brooks of Vinci apparently served Leonardo well. His attention to natural detail in the shimmering hair of the dog and the minute scales of the fish stand out from the rest of the painting. Even at a young age, Leonardo seems to have had an innate ability to capture the detail of nature — a skill he would perfect over his career.

Detail of "*Tobias and the Angel,* Andrea del Verrochio, c. 1470; the fish and dog were likely painted by a young Leonardo — {{PD-1923}}

Tobias and the Angel dates to around 1470. It is amazing to think that in just four years of training, Leonardo could paint as well as he did. Of course, he was just getting started. Andrea must have seen Leonardo's talent, because he immediately had his young apprentice help with more paintings. Within two more years, Leonardo da Vinci became an official, professional painter.

This momentous occasion happened when he joined the confraternity (a professional club) of the Florentine painters. The *Compagnia di San Luca* was an important professional organization to which the most important Renaissance artists of the day belonged. On July 1, 1472, the secretary of the confraternity scribbled the name of "Lyonardo di Ser Piero da Vinci" into the membership books and next to it, the title of *dipintore* (painter). Leonardo had to pay 32 gold coins for membership, but it was worth it.

Joining the *Compagnia* was an important moment, and it placed the 20-year old Leonardo on more equal footing with his master, Andrea. After all, the very same day that Leonardo was granted membership, Andrea himself joined the club! From that day onwards, although Leonardo remained a part of Andrea's studio for several more years, it would be in a somewhat different capacity than as an apprentice. Gone were the days of running errands and doing the grunt work of the studio. Although not yet equal to Andrea, Leonardo would now begin to develop his own style as an artist; and about a year after joining the *Compagnia*, he got the chance to paint his very own painting.[42]

---

42. Nicholl, Charles. *Leonardo Da Vinci: Flights of the Mind*. New York, NY: Penguin, 2005. Print, 98.

Fun Fact

The *Compagnia di San Luca* was named after Saint Luke, who is the patron saint of painters. He got that title because he is said to have painted a portrait of the living Virgin Mary. The Catholic Church has a lot of patron saints — important individuals who are said to have special care for different types of people. For example, who is the patron saint of students? There are several, including St. Scholastica, St. Augustine, and St. Thomas Aquinas.

About the same year he sat on the Tuscan hillside drawing the summer scene before him in 1473, Leonardo completed his first full painting. It's unfortunate that we don't know more about the background to this important piece, which is now known as the *Madonna of the Carnation*.

Around this time, Andrea's studio was producing several of these small paintings of the Virgin Mary holding the infant Jesus, and another one of his apprentices, Leonardo's friend, Lorenzo di Credi, had painted one a year or so earlier. Called "devotionals," these paintings were done on small wooden panels only about two feet tall and one-and-a-half feet wide. Wealthy individuals and religious orders purchased these devotionals to gaze at when praying.[43]

No one is quite sure who commissioned the *Madonna of the Carnation* from Andrea's studio, but the master felt confident enough in Leonardo's ability to give the project entirely to him. Like in his touch to the *Tobias and the Angel*, Leonardo expertly depicts nature in this small devotional (look at the soaring mountain-scape shown through the window behind Mary).

---

43. Zöllner, Frank et. al. *Leonardo da Vinci: the Complete Paintings.* Köln: Taschen, 2011. Print, 13-14.

Madonna of the Carnation, Leonardo da Vinci, c. 1473 — {{PD-1923}}

This painting also reveals the very beginning of what would become a mark of Leonardo's style: the realistic depiction of human figures. It would help to compare Leonardo's take on the scene with another contemporary artist.

Look at Lorenzo di Credi's painting of the same scene in his *Madonna of the Pomegranate* (also known as the *Dreyfus Madonna*).

"Dreyfus Madonna (Madonna of the Pomegranate),
Lorenzo di Credi, c. 1480 — {{PD-1923}}

The infant Jesus is standing on Mary's lap (certainly not something a real baby would do) and looks somewhat stiff and awkward. It almost looks like the infant Jesus is just a small adult, rather than an actual baby.

Now turning to Leonardo's painting, Jesus, shown in all the pudgy cuteness of a real baby, sits on Mary's lap and curiously reaches towards the red carnation flower she holds in her hand. Anyone who has held a baby in real life knows that any jewelry or clothing within reach of their pudgy little hands is not safe. Babies are curious about everything! Not only has Leonardo drawn the infant in a realistic manner, but in a realistic pose as well — one that is touchingly authentic. For the rest of his career, Leonardo would strive to perfect the depiction of his human subjects, spending long hours sketching and drawing from real life models.

A ROUGH START

Four years after he completed the *Madonna of the Carnation*, Leonardo decided to start a new chapter in his life. He prepared to leave Andrea's studio and to create one of his own. He had been with Andrea for over 10 years, first as an apprentice and then as a sort of associate painter. Now, he would be an equal. He had at least a few full paintings to his name (including the *Madonna of the Carnation* and others besides), lots of hands-on experience with other aspects of Renaissance art, and the connections he had made through Andrea to some wealthy and important clients, including Lorenzo de'Medici. The stars were aligned, Leonardo thought, and so he set off.

He didn't go far, ending up somewhere near Andrea's own studio. He had taken his first step toward a new life, though — a young *maestro* entering the crowded field of the Florentine art market. As he would do several times in his life, Leonardo began building up his own studio, surrounding himself with a new family. No sooner did he set up shop than he took on apprentices of his own. One of the earliest ones was a young man named Paolo. Unfortunately, for Leonardo, Paolo didn't last long; the young man got into trouble with the Florentine authorities and had to leave town fast. Right from the beginning, Leonardo had a way of picking strange friends and associates.

Even though Poalo's abrupt exit left him a little short on help, Leonardo received his first commission as an independent painter in January of 1478. It was a commission from the Signoria, the governing council of Florence, for a large painted panel called an altarpiece, which would be hung in the chapel located in the council building. Leonardo was not the Signoria's first choice for the commission. But another artist had turned down the job the previous month and beggars can't be choosers, thought the council. As far as Leonardo was concerned, even being second-choice for such a prestigious job was a great start for a young professional. The job even came with a cash advance, which would have allowed Leonardo to pay for the supplies for the painting, rather than him having to dip into his own money as many artists had to do.

If Leonardo's early paintings with Andrea showed the skill that he would later master as a painter, this first commission as a professional showed a bad habit that the artist would never quite shake. Despite the prestige of the commission, Leonardo never finished the painting. We don't even know for certain that he started it!

Leonardo da Vinci may have been a genius with the paintbrush, but he had a terrible work ethic.

ASSASSINATIONS

A few months after he had failed to hold up his end of the bargain with the Signoria, Leonardo and the rest of Florence witnessed a major political event that sent shockwaves throughout Renaissance Italy. Following the death of Piero de'Medici in 1469, his son Lorenzo had taken over control of the family business and role as leader of Florence. For years, the Medici had been the bank of the Pope in Rome, lending the pontiff money whenever he needed it.

That relationship quickly turned sour when Pope Sixtus IV della Rovere asked Lorenzo to lend him money so that he could fund his nephew's conquest of the nearby city of Imola. Lorenzo, skeptical of the Pope's intentions, denied him the loan. Of course, the Pope was furious and quickly dissolved his accounts with the Medici and entered into a partnership with Lorenzo's rivals, the Pazzi.

The Pazzi family in Florence, the Pope in Rome, and several other people elsewhere conspired to assassinate Lorenzo and take over power in Florence. The result was the Pazzi Conspiracy of April 1478, in which assassins dressed as priests attempted to kill Lorenzo and his younger brother, Giuliano, while they celebrated Easter Mass in church. Although taken completely by surprise, Lorenzo fought his way clear of the assassins, but his brother was killed. Thinking they had accomplished the deed, the conspirators rode through Florence shouting, "Liberty!" and thought that the people would rise with them in rejoicing the overthrow of the Medici.

All of Lorenzo's work in making the people of Florence happy paid off, though, and when Lorenzo himself appeared to the people unharmed, the city revolted against the conspirators.[44] This began a year-long spectacle of public executions, the conspirators scurrying from the hangman's noose like rats from a cat. Leonardo himself attended at least one of the hangings, joining the crowd of onlookers as one of the assassins, Bernardo di

---

44. Bartlett, Kenneth R. *A Short History of the Italian Renaissance*. Toronto: Toronto UP, 2013, Print, 109.

Bandino, was hanged in December of 1479. Always carrying his sketch-book with him, Leonardo drew Bandino hanging from the window of a building in the heart of Florence, the quick sketch preserved now in one of his notebooks.[45]

"Sketch of hanged assassin Bernardo di Bandino found among the pages of Leonardo's notebooks — {{PD-1923}}"]]

45. Nicholl, Charles. *Leonardo Da Vinci: Flights of the Mind.* New York, NY: Penguin, 2005. Print, 140.

Don't Just Take my Word for It!

Renaissance Florence might have been a joyous place during public festivals, but it was also brutal during times of political unrest. In his 1532 book *History of Florence and the Affairs of Italy*, Niccolò Machiavelli describes the terrible scene following the collapse of the Pazzi Conspiracy:

". . . the whole city was roused to arms . . . the name of the Medici echoed everywhere, and portions of dead bodies were seen borne on spears and scattered through the streets; while everyone was transported with rage against the Pazzi and pursued them with relentless cruelty. The people took possession of their houses, and Francesco [one of the conspirators] . . . was led to the palace and hanged beside . . . the rest."[46]

The whole conspiracy and subsequent war between Florence, the Pope in Rome, and the Pope's allies throughout Italy proved far more important to Leonardo's life than a simple sketch in a notebook. Shortly after the attempted coup, the young leader of the nearby city of Milan, Ludovico Sforza, visited Lorenzo de'Medici in Florence to offer him his condolences over the murder of his brother. He also came with an offer of aid in the coming war. This alliance created a bridge between the two great cities of Florence and Milan, one that Leonardo would cross over in the pursuit of his goals.

The unstoppable flow of fate was conspiring once more to sweep Leonardo da Vinci along its path, this time taking him further afield than ever before.

---

46. Machiavelli, Niccolò. *History of Florence and the Affairs of Italy*. N.p.: Public Domain, 2001. Electronic, 379-380

CHAPTER 5

New Beginnings

*I*taly had definitely seen more spectacular debuts than Leonardo da Vinci's.

At 25 years old, Leonardo entered the art scene his own master in 1477. He opened his own studio, sought out his own apprentices, and settled into a life he hoped would be as successful as Andrea Verrocchio's. It even looked like his hopes had become reality when he won the prestigious commission from the Signoria in 1478 to paint an altarpiece. But, if he learned how to actually paint under Andrea, he certainly didn't learn how to operate a business. In an industry where success relied on a good reputation, Leonardo quickly developed one for being difficult to work with by breaking his contract and not finishing the altarpiece.

Thankfully for the young artist, he fended off poverty by landing a few more commissions later that year, despite yet another outbreak of the plague and the ongoing turmoil of the Pazzi Conspiracy. One of the more important jobs he got was to paint the portrait of Ginevra de' Benci, the daughter of a wealthy banking family in Florence and an acquaintance of Lorenzo de'Medici himself. The end result, according to an early biographer of Leonardo, was "a work of such finish that it appeared not to be a portrait but Ginevra in person." [47] Looking back, the portrait of Ginevra

---

47. Bramly, Serge. *Leonardo: The Artist and the Man.* London: Penguin, 1994. Print, 150.

was early practice for one of Leonardo's most famous works of all: the *Mona Lisa*. But that great masterpiece lingered on the horizon years away.

Ginevra de' Benci, Leonardo da Vinci, c. 1478; bears a striking resemblance to his later, more famous portrait of Lisa del Giocondo known as *Mona Lisa* — {{PD-1923}}

Fun Fact

One of Leonardo's unfinished paintings, dating to around 1480, is known as *Saint Jerome* and was discovered completely by accident in the early 1800s by none other than the uncle of the famous French Emperor, Napoleon Bonaparte. One day while walking the streets of Rome, Bonaparte's uncle entered a pawnshop and saw at the back a small wood cupboard. On closer inspection, the cupboard had an extraordinary door. The door, it turned out, was a portion of Leonardo's *Saint Jerome*, which had been cut up and reused over the years! Hoping to discover the other half of the painting, Bonaparte's uncle finally found it months later. A local shoemaker had been using it as a table. [48]

His successful completion of the Ginevra portrait could have been an important step in fixing his poor reputation. You really can't say that Leonardo didn't have chances to succeed — it's just that he kept sabotaging himself! True to form, no sooner did he finish with Ginevra than he went back to his old habit of leaving projects half-finished. By 1481, Leonardo was desperate for work and his prospects were poor. If he couldn't rely on his reputation, then he would have to find other ways of surviving. If he had picked up anything during his time with Andrea it was the importance of knowing the right people. Just like today, in Renaissance Italy it wasn't what you knew, but who you knew, that determined your success.

Leonardo might have been lazy with his deadlines those early years of his career, but he certainly hadn't been sitting idle.

---

48. Ibid. 153.

NEW FRIENDS, NEW HORIZONS

In the 10 years he spent with Andrea's studio, Leonardo had made acquaintances with some of the brightest stars of the Italian Renaissance. From painters and sculptors to poets and philosophers, the young Leonardo mingled with them all. Starting his own studio, he now continued to expand his network. Soon, he became more and more embedded in the city of Florence, gradually making his way closer to the center of power: Lorenzo de'Medici.

Shortly after opening his own workshop, Leonardo took time away from the studio to seek out the great thinkers of the day. In one of his notebooks, he wrote the names of five men who he had either met or wished to meet. Of the five, only one was a painter; the rest were scientists or philosophers. One of the most important names on the list was Carlo Marmocchi, an engineer and mathematician in the service of the Signoria. We don't know if Leonardo ever became close to Marmocchi, but he certainly learned from the man.

More importantly, Leonardo's acquaintance with the engineer marks the beginning of his own personal fascination with machines. Around this same time, Leonardo began drawing the first of his fantastical engineering devices in the margins of his notebooks. When he probably should have been working on his painting commissions, he instead spent hours devising machines for lifting and moving heavy objects and many other purposes.[49]

If he might not have been especially close to the engineer Marmocchi, he certainly was close to an older man named Antonio Cammelli, also known as "Il Pistoiese," or "The Pistoan" (Pistoa was a town near Florence). Cam-

---

49. Nicholl, Charles. *Leonardo Da Vinci: Flights of the Mind*. New York, NY: Penguin, 2005. Print, 150.

melli was a poet of some renown whose style of language was something new to Italy. Rather than writing in fancy language, Cammelli preferred slang, and his poems are often comical in a bawdy sort of way (think spoofy songs on Saturday Night Live instead of boring operas at the theater).

Don't Just Take my Word for It!

A Cardinal of the Catholic Church named Bibbiena summarized Cammelli's poetic style as "jokes, salt, and honey." Here is a short bit of one of Cammelli's poems, just to give you a taste:

"So take a good look at me all who wish: how ugly a man looks when he has no money."

Okay, I never said his poetry was very happy. But then again, living in a world of war, plague, and poverty takes its toll on people. Taking a more optimistic look on the subject, Cammelli later writes:

"Don't despise me because I'm poor: a man is poor when he desires many things."

Leonardo met the middle-aged Cammelli sometime in the late 1470s. Poets, like painters, sought the patronage of the wealthy and powerful, and the two men probably met while running in the same social circles.

They hit it off right away. Cammelli's sense of humor mingled well with Leonardo's. And although he never seemed to have cared for poetry before, once he met Cammelli, Leonardo's notebooks suddenly fill with snippets of poems. Several of Cammelli's poems, written in his own hand, were found in Leonardo's notebooks, proof of their close friendship. One poem was even addressed to Leonardo himself, written in 1479. Unfortunately, we'll never know exactly what the comical poet had to say about Leonardo because the short poem is obscured by a large ink stain.[50]

These were the people, then, who Leonardo surrounded himself with during the first few years of his professional career. Scientists, engineers, poets, painters — an eclectic group of friends! If Leonardo did not already have a thirst for knowledge, he soon developed one. For the young man, each person he met provided him yet another opportunity to learn something new. Leonardo's education never ended. There was a downside, of course. These flights of fancy were sometimes enjoyed at the expense of his actual work. After all, he was being paid to paint, not write poems and draw fanciful machines.

There was an upside to this socializing, though: Leonardo was developing a crucial list of professional contacts. These contacts would prove important because, like moths flittering around a lightbulb, all his new friends were irresistibly drawn to the one great benefactor of the city: Lorenzo de'Medici. All Leonardo had to do was find a way into the Medici inner circle, where all the money and prestige lay.[51]

LEONARDO AND LORENZO

Over the course of his apprenticeship with Andrea, Leonardo had a few opportunities to meet the great Medici. However, as a lowly apprentice among a studio full of them, he had been unmemorable to Lorenzo. More likely, the two became remotely acquainted when Leonardo had taken on the Ginevra de' Benci commission in 1478 or 1479. Lorenzo also liked to surround himself with writers, philosophers, and artists, and he was always

---

50. Ibid 153-154.
51. Burke, Peter. *The Italian Renaissance: Culture and Society in Italy*. Cambridge: Polity, 2014. Print, 102.

on the search for new talent. Perhaps this Leonardo da Vinci could be one of them?

That, at least was Leonardo's ambition. In just a short few years, he had learned the struggles of life as a freelance artist. It took time and money to establish a studio, and then you still had to go out and search for work. Some artists resigned themselves to producing small paintings of popular subjects and selling them in front of their studios to people walking by. This was the lowest a painter could go, and it was not something Leonardo wanted to have to do. But if it made the difference between eating one week and starving the next, then he might just have to swallow his pride and do it. Once an artist received a commission, there was no guarantee he would get the money when he needed it. Payment wasn't always given up front. Sometimes clients paid out in installments as the artist completed separate phases of the work. At other times, the clients kept the money until the work was finally delivered to them. Sometimes payment wasn't even in the form of cash money, but in property or other goods.[52]

Don't Just Take my Word for It!

Writing shortly after Leonardo's death, the great biographer and artist, Giorgio Vasari, once remarked, "The artist today struggles to ward off famine rather than to win fame, and this crushes and buries his talent and obscures his name." And Benvenuto di Giovanni, an artist from Sienna, wrote in 1488, "The gains in our profession are slight and limited, because little is produced and less earned."[53]

---

52. Ibid. 116.
53. Ibid. 86.

For a Renaissance artist, a paycheck was never a guaranteed thing. That's why so many artists and other men of great talent sought out the attentions of wealthy and powerful rulers like Lorenzo de'Medici. Rather than paying artists by each piece completed, many rulers like Lorenzo would keep artists "on retainer," meaning they would pay them a consistent salary. All the artist had to do in return was work on projects at the ruler's request.

That was the kind of working relationship Leonardo hoped to secure with Lorenzo, and an opening presented itself in 1481. Pope Sixtus IV, who had reconciled his differences with Lorenzo following the failed Pazzi Conspiracy, asked Lorenzo to send him Florence's best painters. The Pope had built a beautiful new chapel in Rome — the Sistine Chapel — and he needed painters to decorate it. Lorenzo often sent artists around Italy as ambassadors of sorts (art was, after all, Florence's greatest export), and he would give their talents to fellow rulers as gifts and as a means of securing alliances. He had sent Andrea Verrocchio to nearby Pistoia to build a monument for that city's ruler and had lent the services of a famous architect to the King of Naples. Now, the Pope wanted a piece of the pie.

The city was agog with excitement. Who would Lorenzo send to Rome, a city that had new building projects every year? For the artists chosen, it would be an opportunity to make a name for themselves. And for Lorenzo, it would be a chance to solidify his relationship with the Pope — a man who had conspired to kill him just three years earlier. He had to choose wisely!

Lorenzo needed to put his best foot forward. Unfortunately, for Leonardo, his poor reputation conspired against him, and Lorenzo knew he couldn't send an artist who never finished paintings. It was quite a blow to Leonardo to see several of his companions — Botticcelli, Signorelli, and Perugino — set off for Rome without him. Leonardo hadn't made the cut.

FINAL STRAW

When Lorenzo overlooked him for the mission to Rome, Leonardo got the message loud and clear: Lorezno de'Medici was not his ticket to success. As a sort of apology for ignoring him, Lorenzo offered a different job to Leonardo: the task of restoring broken statues at his estate. It came with a paycheck, but no prestige. Leonardo, the rising star of Florentine art, was now a repairman.[54]

Unfortunately, things got even more difficult for the struggling artist. He became so desperate that he turned to an unlikely source for help. Leonardo went to his father.

Just as he had secured his son the apprenticeship with Andrea through his business contacts, Piero hoped to find his son a prospective client who would help heal the young man's poor reputation.

What he found was a huge headache.

One of Piero's notarial clients was the monastery of San Donato at Scopeto, which agreed to commission a painting of a biblical scene from Leonardo. But there were some huge strings attached. According to the contract written up by the monastery, Leonardo had to complete the painting "within twenty-four months, or at the most within thirty months; and in case of not finishing it he forfeits whatever he has done of it, and it is our right to do what we want with it." Apparently, Leonardo's reputation for not finishing works had gotten around, and the monastery wasn't taking any chances. The weirdest thing about the contract wasn't the deadline, though, but the payment. Leonardo was to be paid in the form of a piece of property in the countryside that had been willed to the monastery by a man named Simone.

---

54. Bramly, Serge. *Leonardo: The Artist and the Man*. London: Penguin, 1994. Print, 156.

Sounds pretty good, right? Well, not really. You see, before he could take the piece of property, the contract stipulated that Leonardo would have to pay 150 gold florins to a young girl who had been the friend of Simone. The property was only worth 300. On top of all of that, the contract made it clear that Leonardo also had to pay for all the supplies necessary to create the painting itself.[55] So in the end, the most he could hope for would be 150 florins minus the cost of supplies. Leonardo found himself between a rock and a hard place. He had few alternatives. He took the commission, but he started looking elsewhere for work.

Then it dawned on him: a whole wide world awaited him beyond the walls of Florence. He had to leave the city of his youth and seek his destiny elsewhere.

Fun Fact

While he was struggling to work on the painting for the monastery San Donato at Scopeto, Leonardo had to take small jobs to make ends meet. He was paid several carts' full of firewood for painting the clock at the monastery. He got so desperate by the end of summer 1481 that he borrowed grain from the monastery, which the monks sought payment for later. No wonder he sought new horizons![56]

55. Nicholl, Charles. *Leonardo Da Vinci: Flights of the Mind*. New York, NY: Penguin, 2005. Print, 168.
56. Ibid. 169.

A NEW ADVENTURE

Leonardo's entire world had centered on Florence and the surrounding countryside of his youth — an area of perhaps 100 square miles. When he left Andrea's workshop in 1477, he probably intended to stay in the city for years to come. Florence was, after all, the center of the Renaissance and the best place for a professional painter to ply his trade. By fall of 1481, though, Leonardo was approaching 30 years on this earth and, in his mind, had little to show for it. After about five years as an independent artist, he found himself saddled with a difficult commission, one that had no hope for money in sight. Lorenzo, the one man who could have raised him out of obscurity, had overlooked him, perhaps because of Leonardo's poor reputation. The job of restoring old statues at the Medici estate was a poor substitute and only added insult to injury.

Leonardo looked for an exit, and he found it in an unlikely place.

Following the Pazzi Conspiracy, the cities of Milan and Florence had grown closer. Like his relationship with the Pope, Lorenzo looked to solidify the one he had with Ludovico Sforza, the uncle and regent to the boy Duke of Milan. He again sent for his collection of artist-ambassadors. This time, Leonardo needed to get a spot on the team of artists any way he could. So, rather than compete with the other painters — an exercise in futility since Lorenzo had made it clear that he did not see Leonardo as a very skilled painter — Leonardo offered his service as a musician.

That's right, a musician. But it's not as bizarre as it seems. From a very early age, Leonardo had shown great talent for music. He could sing beautifully and played many instruments, including the lyre (a kind of early violin). Sometime in the late 1470s, Leonardo had designed a beautiful lyre, built partially of silver. The instrument was designed in the shape of a horse's head and was expertly crafted "so that the sound would be more full and resonant."[57] Lorenzo, knowing that Ludovico Sforza loved music and live performances, agreed that Leonardo da Vinci be sent to Milan.

A WHOLE NEW WORLD

However, Milan was no Florence. For one, the city had been in chaos for the past generation. Whereas the Medici had been able to maintain relatively peaceful power over Florence for decades, Milan of the mid-1400s was ripped apart by cruel rulers and civil war.

At the same time that Lorenzo's grandfather, Cosimo, ascended to power in Florence, Milan's ruling dynasty of dukes came to an end with no heirs in sight. This left a power vacuum, with the throne up for grabs. The son-in-law of the last duke sought to get control of the city. His name was Francesco Sforza. The name "Sforza" means "strong" in Italian, which suited Francesco quite well. Broad-shouldered and standing tall, Francesco had risen through the ranks of ambitious Milanese to become the most feared military general of his day. For a time, he had been a mercenary, a *condotiere*, and fought for Florence as well as Milan. After marrying the daughter of the Duke of Milan, he settled down. When the old duke died, Francesco sprang once more into action, eventually winning the seat of power in 1450 and ruling until his death in 1466. His heir, Galeazzo Maria, was a cruel ruler and was assassinated in 1476 while attending church (just like the Pazzi tried to do to Lorenzo a few years later in Florence).

Galeazzo left his seven-year-old son in charge — hardly a great situation for the city. A brief struggle ensued to determine who would be the child's regent, a position whose job it was to assist the boy-ruler until he could take over the position himself. His uncle, Ludovico Sforza, won out.

---

57. Vasari, Giorgio. *The Lives of the Artists*. Trans. Julia C. Bondanella and Peter Bondanella. New York: Oxford UP, 1991. Print, 289.

Ludovico Sforza was nicknamed "Il Moro" (the Moor) because of his dark skin; while his nephew grew up, he would essentially be the ruler of Milan.[58]

Therefore, it was from Ludovico that Leonardo would now hope to secure his future. And so, shouldering his lyre, the great painter left the city of his youth and, he hoped, his troubles behind.

---

58. Bartlett, Kenneth R. *A Short History of the Italian Renaissance*. Toronto: Toronto UP, 2013, Print, 183.

CHAPTER 6

Leonardo in Milan

*I*n February of 1482, Leonardo da Vinci found himself outside the great walls of Florence once more. This was a sight that, as a 14-year-old arriving for his apprenticeship, had filled him with giddy anticipation. Now it left him feeling forlorn. This time, he was leaving Florence behind, possibly never to return. But what could have been a sad three-week trek to the northern city of Milan, actually ended up being joyful.

It always helps to have good traveling companions.

In a role that he had unfortunately become used to, Leonardo was one of the least important people taking the 188-mile trip. At the head of the party were Bernardo Rucellai and Pier Francesco da San Miniato, Florentine politicians and official ambassadors. These men would be the voice of Lorenzo de'Medici, relaying messages from their ruler to Ludovico Sforza and vice versa. They weren't the usual stuffy sort of politicians, though, and they got along well with the boisterous artist-musician with his funny-looking lyre. Leonardo enjoyed their company. [59]

On more equal footing with Leonardo were Atalante Migliorotti and Tommaso di Giovanni Masini. Atalante was another musician and 10 years

59. Nicholl, Charles. *Leonardo Da Vinci: Flights of the Mind.* New York, NY: Penguin, 2005. Print, 177-78.

Leonardo's junior. He was headed to Milan as another artist-ambassador for Florence. A handsome youth with long curly hair, Atalante proved to be the perfect model for Leonardo, who drew portraits of him in his note-books.[60] Tommaso, on the other hand . . . Well, he was another character entirely. A few years younger than Leonardo, he was born just outside of Florence. The son of a gardener, the young man claimed he was the illegit-imate son of none other than the brother-in-law of Lorenzo de'Medici. This was quite a claim to make no matter the circumstances. It was an es-pecially awkward claim to make on this journey, since Lorenzo's brother-in-law happened to be Bernardo Rucellai himself! How the ambassador took to the young man's claim of being his illegitimate son wasn't recorded, but we can imagine it would have made for interesting dinners around the campfire!

Did I also mention that Tommaso was a huge jokester? His claim of famil-ial ties was probably just one big gag to him. He happened to be on this journey in the role of Leonardo's apprentice. Or his assistant. Or just his friend. We really don't know. You see, Tommaso is kind of a ghost in the historical record. At any one time in the decades Leonardo knew him, he appears in the records as an engineer, a palm-reader, and an artist's assis-tant. Like Cammelli the poet, Tommaso's sense of humor and mischievous-ness fit well with Leonardo's own wild side. Over the course of the trip to Milan, Leonardo and Tommaso told each other jokes, some of which Leonardo recorded in his notebooks. They are a little vulgar — proving that his time with the bawdy poet Cammelli hadn't been the best influence on the artist![61]

Leonardo therefore enjoyed the three-week trek to Milan with a pretty eclectic group of people. He spent his idle time sketching the handsome

60. Bramly, Serge. *Leonardo: The Artist and the Man*. London: Penguin, 1994. Print, 173.
61. Nicholl, Charles. *Leonardo Da Vinci: Flights of the Mind*. New York, NY: Penguin, 2005. Print, 141.

Atalante, telling jokes with Tommaso, and watching the jokester jest with his supposed father, Bernardo, while in camp. All of these activities were the perfect diversions for Leonardo, who had just entered a new and unknown chapter in his life. What lay ahead was anyone's guess. He hoped, at least, that it would be better than what he had left behind.

THE CITY OF ST. AMBROSE

The group of Florentines entered the city through the grand Porta Romana, a massive gate decorated in marble sculptures depicting scenes from Milan's great history.[62] Once through the gate, the cacophony of sounds and smells of a city in celebration swallowed Leonardo and his companions. It just so happened they had arrived during the festival week of St. Ambrose, the famous church leader who had called the city home centuries earlier. The pageantry of a city in celebration made Leonardo and the other Florentines feel right at home. I guess Milan wasn't so different from Florence after all![63]

As they wound their way through the city, though, the differences became clearer. Leonardo struggled to understand the people they passed. He was in Lombardy now, the northernmost region of Italy, and the dialect the people spoke was far different from what Leonardo was used to.[64] Milan was also larger than Florence — by about 20,000 people — and was one of the largest cities in the western world.[65]

---

62. Ibid 187.
63. Ibid. 189.
64. Ibid. 193.
65. Lubkin, Gregory. *A Renaissance Court: Milan Under Galeazzo Maria Sforza*. Berkeley: University of California Press, 1994. Print, 5.

While Florence had passed through the centuries of warfare generations earlier, Milan was still in the midst of civil strife.[66] Leonardo had entered a fortified city, and the dominating bulk of Castello Sforzesco loomed over everything. Built up over the past few years, the Castello (castle) was "beautiful and very strong . . . surrounded by ditches, covering half a square mile or more, with a walled garden about three miles in perimeter," as one eyewitness described it.[67]

Since they were on official business from Florence, Leonardo and his group made their way through the city towards the Castello. They had a date with Ludovico, where Leonardo would have a chance to make a good first impression on the man he hoped would be his new patron.

A Recipe for Success

Sometimes, Leonardo learned from his mistakes. At least he tried to. Just before leaving Florence, the young painter had taken stock of his situation. He knew he was headed for Milan, a city run by a strong-man who came from a long line of military generals. He knew also that the city and surrounding region featured some impressive fortifications. Somewhere in that knowledge lay the key to success, and Leonardo thought he had found it.

While the diplomats Bernardo and Pier had in hand official dispatches from Lorenzo, Leonardo had a letter. More than a letter. Leonardo carried a personal resume, or cover letter, laying out his qualifications. The artist hoped that Ludovico would find in it something that would make him worth keeping around. The letter read, in part:

---

66. Ady, Cecilia M. *A History of Milan under the Sforza*. N.p.: Methuen, 1907. Print. 157

67. Nicholl, Charles. *Leonardo Da Vinci: Flights of the Mind*. New York, NY: Penguin, 2005. Print, 187.

"Most Illustrious Lord . . . I shall endeavor . . . to reveal my secrets to Your Excellency, for whom I offer to execute, at your convenience, all the items briefly noted below.

1. *I have a model of very strong but light bridges, extremely easy to carry, by means of which you will be able to pursue . . . an enemy; I have others, which are sturdy and will resist fire as well as attack, and are easy to lay down and take up. I also know ways to burn and destroy those of the enemy.*

2. *During a siege, I know how to dry up the water of the moats and how to construct an infinite number of bridges, covered ways, scaling ladders, and other machines for this type of enterprise.*

3. *I also have models of mortars that are very practical and easy to transport, with which I can project stones so that they seem to be raining down and their smoke will plunge the enemy into terror, to his great hurt and confusion.*

4. *And if battle is to be joined at sea, I have many very efficient machines for both attack and defense; and vessels that will resist even the heaviest cannon fire, fumes, and gunpowder."*

The letter goes on and on, each new item on the list more fantastical than the last.

We know Leonardo had an interest in engineering before and had some practical experience with it during his time in Andrea's studio, but it's doubtful he was able to execute even half of the things he promised Ludovico in his letter. What on earth was Leonardo's game here? Well, in part, he was trying to reinvent himself as a military engineer. Having failed to attract the attention of one ruler with his painting skills, he now hoped to attract Ludovico with what he thought the duke would want most: military capabilities. The sly Leonardo had an ulterior motive, though. Buried at the end of the letter, almost as an after-thought, Leonardo mentions:

> *"I can carry out sculpture in marble, bronze, and clay; and in painting can do any kind of work as well as any man, whoever he be.*
>
> *Moreover, the bronze horse could be made that will be to the immortal glory and eternal honor of the lord your father of blessed memory and of the illustrious house of Sforza."*

Herein lay Leonardo's true hopes for Milan. It had gotten around Italy that Ludovico wanted to commission a larger-than-life size bronze sculpture of his father, Francesco Sforza (the famous general-turned-Milanese Duke). Since the ancient Romans, statues of emperors or victorious generals on horseback were the pinnacle of imperial public art. The talent it required to not only sculpt the image but to engineer it so that the weight of the statue itself (man and horse combined) didn't cause the whole thing to fall apart was extraordinary.

Now, Ludovico wanted one just like those from the ancient past, this time featuring his father. Such a public display would honor his father's memory and the memory of the Sforza family. The statue had to be big, bigger than any that had been built before, requiring a special kind of talent. The artist who won this commission would become world-famous. Enter Leonardo da Vinci.

By dangling bits of enticing engineering projects in front of Ludovico in his letter, Leonardo hoped to get the ruler's attention. But he buried the true hope for his future in Milan: to win the commission for the biggest public statue in all of Italy. But what if Ludovico requested Leonardo make good on his lofty claims of military skill? Well, Leonardo would have to "fake it 'till he made it."[68]

LEONARDO AND LUDOVICO

Arriving through the gate of the Castello Sforzesco, the group of Florentines found themselves in yet another large courtyard (size mattered to Ludovico). From there they exited into a smaller courtyard and finally into a reception room of sorts. Standing amid the group of messengers, administrators, and hangers-on that orbit every person of power, Ludovico Sforza watched this strange group of foreigners approach.

As he had inherited his family's size, Ludovico "The Moor" was broad-shouldered and tall, although a bit pudgy. He was a different kind of ruler than Lorenzo de'Medici. Lorenzo knew he was in charge of Florence, but his power was subtle and behind-the-scenes. This was not the case for Ludovico. A popular song of the day sums up Ludovico's idea of his own importance:

> *"I said there was one God in Heaven*
> *And on earth one Moor*
> *At my good will and pleasure*
> *I made peace and war."*[69]

When Leonardo finally presented his beautifully crafted horse-head lyre to the man, he hoped Ludovico was in a mood to make peace, not war. Thankfully for Leonardo, "The Moor" immediately loved the young Florentine's music. It helped, too, that Leonardo had developed a talent for oratory during his time hobnobbing with the elite of Florence. One person

---

68. Bramly, Serge. *Leonardo: The Artist and the Man*. London: Penguin, 1994. Print, 174-176.
69. Ibid. 200.

remarked that "Leonardo was so pleasing in his conversation that he won everyone's heart." Standing up among the crowd in the reception hall, the artist-turned-musician showed off his talent, reciting speeches from history and bits of poetry (hopefully not from his friend Cammelli!). He won over Ludovico from the start. It was later recorded that "When the duke had listened to the admirable arguments of Leonardo, he became so enamoured of his abilities that it was incredible to behold."[70]

After these theatricals and a brief introduction, Leonardo passed his resume to Ludovico outlining his grand skills of military engineering (Oh, and also the notice that he could certainly be the artist to design that statue of Ludovico's father).

The seed had been planted. Now, all Leonardo had to do was wait for it to take root.

GETTING SETTLED

Maybe remembering his earlier difficulty in setting up a studio in Florence, Leonardo didn't immediately begin one in Milan. Instead, after meeting Ludovico, he shacked up with the de Predis brothers, a family of fellow artists. The eldest of the brothers, Cristoforo, worked chiefly as an illuminator, producing wonderfully delicate miniature illustrations for books and other detailed work. His younger half-brother, Ambrogio, also excelled as a miniaturist but became an accomplished painter of portraits as well. The other four brothers were accomplished in a variety of other art forms, making the de Predis studio capable of completing almost any commission sent its way. Best of all, for someone like Leonardo, the de Predis were well connected to the Milanese court and Ludovico in particular. They were the

70. Vasari, Giorgio. *The Lives of the Artists*. Trans. Julia C. Bondanella and Peter Bondanella. New York: Oxford UP, 1991. Print, 289.

perfect people to show Leonardo the ropes in Milan while he continued to develop his own relationship with Il Moro.[71]

Joining Leonardo in the de Predis apartments were Atalante and, of course, Tommaso. For the next few years, this was Leonardo's home as he navigated the waters of this new city of opportunities.[72]

The first opportunities that presented themselves looked familiar to Leonardo. The artist might have played down his artistic capabilities in his letter to Ludovico, but he was still known as an accomplished painter. It is no wonder, then, that he found work in that capacity soon after arriving in Milan. In April 1483, Leonardo and two of the de Predis brothers received an important commission from a local fraternity, perhaps at the suggestion of Ludovico himself. For 800 gold coins, the artists were tasked with painting a large altarpiece for display in the fraternity's chapel in the Church of San Francesco Grande. Recognizing the Florentine's skill at painting, the fraternity asked that Leonardo paint the large central panel, leaving the two smaller side panels for the de Predis brothers. The final piece, delivered to the fraternity two years later (Leonardo still couldn't shake his habit of tardiness), is now known as the *Virgin of the Rocks*.[73]

FLIGHTS OF FANCY

The bad habit Leonardo picked up in Florence of getting sidetracked with random projects continued during his time in Milan. As he was working on the *Virgin of the Rocks*, he began fully to devote himself to his notebooks. Up until this point, Leonardo had put down all of his writing and

---

71. Bramly, Serge. *Leonardo: The Artist and the Man*. London: Penguin, 1994. Print, 185
72. Nicholl, Charles. *Leonardo Da Vinci: Flights of the Mind*. New York, NY: Penguin, 2005. Print, 196.
73. Zöllner, Frank et. al. *Leonardo da Vinci: The Complete Paintings*. Köln: Taschen, 2011. Print. 64.

doodles onto loose-leaf, miscellaneous sheets that happened to be lying around. Starting in the mid-1480s, though, he began filling entire books with his thoughts, drawings, and doodles.

In 1485, Milan was in the throes of a three-year outbreak of the plague. The most serious estimates placed the death toll at somewhere near a third of the city's population. There is no doubt that Leonardo himself lost friends or acquaintances to the disease as it swept through all levels of Milanese society. As the plague ravished the city, Leonardo's mind turned towards science. Written in the margins of one of his notebooks, the budding scientist scribbled down a recipe to help prevent the disease:

"Take seed of medicinal darnel
Spirits of wine in cotton
Some white henbane
Some teasel
Seed and root of aconite.
Dry it all. Mix this powder with camphor and it is made."

It's unlikely this concoction helped in any way to prevent the transmission of the plague, but the exercise of devising it helped soothe Leonardo's troubled mind.

Out of the Black Death and morbid recipes came Leonardo's earliest concerted thoughts about human flight. Leonardo wasn't alone in his fascination with flight. In fact, it was a popular topic of theoretical thought in Renaissance Italy. But no one seems to have devoted so much technical thought to the mechanics of flight than Leonardo did. Written in his book, now known as the *Codex Atlanticus*, Leonardo sketched and added specifications for the first parachute known in history. It is unlikely that he ever actually built a life-sized model, but as with many of his mechanical inventions, he might have mocked up models of it.[74]

Leonardo's notebook sketch of the first
known parachute concept — {{PD-1923}}

Fun Fact

In 2000, almost 500 years after Leonardo's death, a London-based skydiver proved that Leonardo's design for the parachute actually worked. Adrian Nicholas slowly drifted one-and-a-half miles down from a hot-air balloon, strapped to a version of the parachute sketched in Leonardo's notebooks.[75]

74. Nicholl, Charles. *Leonardo Da Vinci: Flights of the Mind.* New York, NY: Penguin, 2005. Print, 202, 204.
75. Hartley-Brewer, Julia. "Skydiver Proves Da Vinci Chute Works." The Guardian. Guardian News and Media, 27 June 2000. Web. 26 June 2017.

Surrounded by death and disease, the 35-year-old artist looked upwards and outwards to escape the harsh realities of life. His renewed interest in his personal notebooks and the new fascination with science and theoretical engineering developed alongside his painting skills. Although his sketches and personal ruminations didn't immediately translate to money or prestige, Leonardo knew that a Renaissance artist always needed to develop new and better skills. The world was ever-changing and only those able to adapt to the times would come out on top.

LEONARDO THE ENGINEER — ALMOST

Not all of Leonardo's studies in mechanics concerned something as unlikely as human flight. After all, Leonardo had introduced himself to Ludovico as an engineer first and an artist second. His expansive list of engineering capabilities wasn't entirely a means to an end either (the end being the commission for the statue of Francesco Sforza on horseback). Leonardo knew that an engineer in Milan could make a name for himself. After all, at the time Leonardo arrived, the city was at war with nearby Venice. Nearly 70 percent of Ludovico's treasury budget went towards his military. Why shouldn't some of that go to this inventive painter-musician-engineer from Florence?[76] At any rate, that's what Leonardo hoped Ludovico would conclude.

In this, he would be disappointed. It doesn't appear that Ludovico ever tapped into the supposed endless supply of inventive projects that Leonardo had introduced to the Milanese ruler. At least, nothing concrete. It is indeed possible that Leonardo was kept on retainer as a consultant of sorts. However, no actual physical products resulted in this relationship beyond a few iron tools Leonardo designed and had made for Ludovico. We only know of one occasion in which Leonardo was *invited* to submit plans for

---

76. Zöllner, Frank et. al. *Leonardo da Vinci: The Complete Paintings*. Köln: Taschen, 2011. Print. 64.

an architectural/engineering project, but the Florentine painter didn't make the cut. If Leonardo had hoped to dazzle Ludovico with skills he thought the ruler would want, it didn't turn out that way.

In the end, the one thing that won over Ludovico was Leonardo da Vinci's unparalleled skill in painting. Lorenzo de'Medici never commissioned a painting from Leonardo and, if his overlooking Leonardo for the mission to Rome was any indication, didn't even think much of the artist's skill. Ludovico Sforza was different.

"GIVE THANKS . . . TO THE GENIUS AND HAND OF LEONARDO"

Probably starting with the commission of the fraternity for the *Virgin of the Rocks*, Ludovico Sforza lent some support to Leonardo, although it took several more years for an official commission to come from him. That changed in 1485, the same year that Leonardo turned his mind from the ongoing plague and began thinking about flight. In a letter to his ambassador in the court of Matthias Corvinus, King of Hungary, Ludovico stated that he had commissioned a painting of the Virgin Mary from Leonardo on the king's behalf: "A figure of Our Lady as beautiful, as superb, and as devout as he knows how to make without sparing any effort." Unfortunately, no traces of the painting exist today.[77]

This was an important step for Leonardo, and the artist appears to have met — if not exceeded — all of Ludovico's expectations. This painting was followed three or four years later by another important commission from Ludovico: a portrait of the ruler's favorite mistress. By now, Leonardo had shown his expertise with portraiture (remember his portrait in Florence of Ginevra de'Benci). He now turned that talent towards the beautiful young

---

77. Kemp, Martin. *Leonardo*. Oxford: Oxford UP, 2011. Print. 264.

figure of Cecilia Gallerani. In the final portrait, Leonardo depicts the young mistress from the waist-up, half-turning to her left. In her hands, she holds a pet ermine, an animal that symbolized purity (ironic given that Cecilia was a mistress). Leonardo's skill in depicting the beauty stunned all who saw the painting. So life-like was the portrait that, later in life, friends asked Cecilia if she could send it to them, since "it would give us the pleasure of seeing your face."[78]

Don't Just Take my Word for It!

A Florentine poet of the day, Bernardo Bellincioni, wrote a sonnet about Leonardo's portrait of Cecilia:

"O Nature how envious you are
Of Vinci who has painted one of your stars,
The beautiful Cecilia, whose lovely eyes
Make the sunlight seem dark shadow

Think this: the more lively and lovely she is,
The more glory you'll get in ages to come.
Give thanks therefore to Ludovico
And to the genius and the hand of Leonardo,
Who both wish to share her with posterity."

By the time he finished Cecilia's portrait in 1489, Leonardo da Vinci had achieved what he wanted. Sometime in the late 1480s, he began work on what he hoped would be his most important work to date: the Sforza horse statue.

He had won the commission.

---

78. Nicholl, Charles. *Leonardo Da Vinci: Flights of the Mind*. New York, NY: Penguin, 2005. Print, 231.

CHAPTER 7

Leonardo the Celebrity

$\mathcal{B}$y 1489 all was well with the world, as far as Leonardo da Vinci was concerned. Enjoying the last seven years in a new city, he found the talents he had developed in Florence suited him well in Milan. Although he had yet to build any actual working machines or physical buildings, Leonardo was probably kept on retainer as an engineer, providing Ludovico with technical advice on new public projects.

And by the end of the 1480s, there were public projects galore. All of Italy was taking a deep breath of fresh air following a decade of war and plague. Milan currently found itself between conflicts and a city that usually spent most of its money on waging war now had an abundance of resources. Money didn't sit long in the bank. For the next several years, Ludovico employed engineers and architects to rebuild and enlarge buildings in Milan and nearby Pavia and Vigevano, two cities under the Moor's control. Gardens were laid out, streets paved for the first time and building fronts ornamented with sculpture. It was during these years of activity that Leonardo appeared on the official records as an engineer for Ludovico. Despite not actually producing any devices on his own, Leonardo's creative mind, coupled with his smooth talking, made him an immediate favorite of his new patron.[79]

---

79. Bramly, Serge. *Leonardo: The Artist and the Man*. London: Penguin, 1994. Print, 215.

After completing high-profile paintings for the King of Hungary and Ludovico's mistress on behalf of the Milanese ruler, Leonardo had established himself as the top painter in the city. However, despite his success with painting, for the next six years Leonardo took a break from the art form.

He had other things on his mind.

The next decade would be at once the happiest of his life — and the most troubling. Leonardo would face peaks of success and depths of despair as he navigated his new life as a famous Renaissance artist.

The Sforza Horse

Somehow, over the years Leonardo had convinced Ludovico to grant him his one true wish: the commission for the Sforza horse statue. This was a big win for the artist. Although he had been trained by Andrea Verrocchio in the art of sculpture, Leonardo was no sculptor. In fact, he was pretty dismissive of the art form. Writing in one of his books, Leonardo once remarked, "Sculpture is less intellectual than painting, and lacks many characteristics of nature."[80] From a man who loved nature, this was a serious insult.

Always more of a painter than a sculptor, Leonardo hit a snag in his plans for the statue almost immediately. His notebooks from this time were riddled with sketches, doodles and drawings of horses and men on horseback. He finally settled on a style he thought would look most majestic in real life: Ludovico's father, Francesco, astride a horse rearing up on its hind legs, its forelegs crashing down onto an enemy soldier lying on the ground. It

80. Suh, H. Anna., ed. *Leonardo's Notebooks: Writing and Art of the Great Master*. New York: Black Dog & Leventhal, 2005. Print, 314.

would be a marvelous statue, full of vibrant activity and truly embodying the martial prowess of the great Sforza family. It would be a statue in a style never seen before.

Too bad it was nearly impossible to execute.

Fun Fact

Statues of men on horseback are known by historians as "equestrian" statues, from the Latin "equus" which means horse.

You see, this was to be a *bronze* statue. There was a very good reason no one had attempted to design a bronze equestrian statue like Leonardo was planning: the weight of the metal required that the statue have solid support. The way Leonardo envisioned his statue would require the full weight of it be supported primarily on the horse's two back legs. Leonardo wasn't the first one to see the fault in his design. Others spotted it immediately. The Florentine ambassador in Milan, Pietro Alamanni (the other two ambassadors who accompanied Leonardo to Milan in 1482 had since left their positions) wrote to Lorenzo de'Medici in July of 1489:

> *"Prince Ludovico is planning to erect a worthy monument to his father, and in accordance with his order Leonardo has been asked to make a model for a large horse in bronze, ridden by Duke Francesco in full armour. As His Excellence has in mind something wonderful, the like of which has never been seen, he has directed me to write to you, to ask if you would kindly send him one or two Florentine artists who specialize*

in this kind of work. It seems to me that although he has given the com-
mission to Leonardo, he is not confident that he will succeed."[81]

Seeing his commission for the horse slipping away from him, Leonardo
quickly changed his plans. Travelling one day to Pavia (one of those cities
that Ludovico was embellishing with engineering projects), Leonardo
sought inspiration from one of the four great equestrian statues on display
in Italy at the time: *Il Regisole* (*The Sun King*). Dating to sometime in the
late Roman period (300's-500's A.D.), the *Sun King* statue depicted a ruler
astride a horse. This horse, unlike Leonardo's design for the Sforza horse,
trotted along with three of his four legs firmly planted on the base.

Sitting down in front of the statue from antiquity, Leonardo jotted down
his thoughts as they came to him:

- *The one in Pavia is to be praised most of all for its movement.*

- *It is more praiseworthy to imitate antiquities than modern things.*

- *Beauty and utility cannot go together, as is shown in castles and in men.*

- *The trot [of the Il Regisole horse] has almost the quality of a free horse.*

- *Where natural vivacity is missing we must supply it artificially.*[82]

This list of stream-of-conscious thought almost sounds like Leonardo was
trying to convince himself of something. This might have been the first real
time that Leonardo was faced with the reality that he was less talented than
he had thought.

---

81. Nicholl, Charles. *Leonardo Da Vinci: Flights of the Mind.* New York, NY: Penguin, 2005. Print, 248.
82. Ibid. 250.

Right from the onset of his career, the young artist had enjoyed the limelight as a talented painter. Although he had struggled to realize his goals of success while in Florence, that was primarily a result of his work ethic than any real issue with his artistic skill. Even when Lorenzo de'Medici snubbed him for the trip to Rome, Leonardo probably understood that it was his poor reputation for getting work done on time that had really done him in. Now, however, he faced an uncomfortable situation. He might have bitten off more than he could chew with this bronze statue. After all, bronze sculpture was no painting.

Sitting there, staring at the great statue in Pavia, Leonardo learned another important life lesson: no one is infallible. Later in life, he would write, "We know very well that errors are better recognized in the works of others than in our own; and that often, while reproving little faults in others, you may ignore great ones in yourself."[83] Here at least, Leonardo had recognized a serious flaw in his own design for the horse. He'd have to suck it up, swallow his pride, and go about redesigning the statue.

After all, this was going to be his greatest work to date.

LEONARDO SETS UP SHOP AGAIN

Having redesigned the equestrian statue to feature the horse trotting instead of rearing up, Leonardo silenced his critics. No more mention was made of other Florentine artists coming to Milan to assist in the building of the statue. The work would be entirely Leonardo's.

In the meantime, the artist would enjoy the limelight and the benefits that came with it. By the time he had been awarded the commission, Leonardo

---

83. Suh, H. Anna., ed. *Leonardo's Notebooks: Writing and Art of the Great Master.* New York: Black Dog & Leventhal, 2005. Print, 388.

had moved out of the house of the de Predis brothers and set up his own studio. This was his second studio in his career — it wouldn't be his last. It was in this studio that he had produced the portrait of Cecilia Gallerani, which would be his last painting for a number of years. Meanwhile, he accumulated apprentices, who assisted him in his other work and, in time, painted their own paintings under his guidance.

Taking on apprentices not only allowed Leonardo to shape the talent of future generations of artists, but also gave him an important source of income. Like his father had paid for his own tutelage under Andrea, each one of the apprentices Leonardo now took on meant more money. For example, for an otherwise unknown apprentice named Galeazzo, Leonardo received five lire a month from Galeazzo's father (a lire was a type of currency that was less than a gold florin).

Fun Fact

Here are the average annual salaries for a range of professions in 15th-century Italy, in lire.

- 3,750 lire: Captain of Milanese infantry (c. 1520 A.D.)

- 400 lire: Silk-weaver in Venice (c. 1450 A.D.)

- 200 lire: Young bank clerk in Florence (c. 1450 A.D)

- 70 lire: Shop-boy in Florence (c. 1450 A.D.)

- 40 lire: Servant in Florence (c. 1450 A.D.)[84]

84. Burke, Peter. *The Italian Renaissance: Culture and Society in Italy*. Cambridge: Polity, 2014, Print, 230.

So, for his apprentice Galeazzo alone, Leonardo made about 60 lire a year from his family — not a bad income when you consider that at any one time Leonardo had several apprentices!

Leonardo continued to work with the de Predis brothers in his new studio and the jokester Tommaso Masini once again entered his orbit. Shortly after opening his Milanese studio, Leonardo moved his entire operation into Milan's Corte Vecchia (Old Court), a series of princely rooms and halls that once housed the city's ruler. When the Sforza took over power, they moved into the Castello Sforzesco, leaving the Corte Vecchia vacant. Having won the commission for the equestrian statue, Leonardo was given the honor of moving his studio into these large rooms — proof positive of Ludovico's favor.[85]

It was shortly after moving into his new home that Leonardo's life turned topsy-turvy with the arrival of a new assistant. Up to this point, Leonardo had surrounded himself with the type of people who make life interesting. From bawdy poets like Cammelli back in Florence to Tommaso Masini the trickster, Leonardo certainly knew how to pick his companions. The newest addition to this troupe was the 10 year-old Giovanni Giacomo di Pietro Caprotti. Leonardo soon found a more appropriate name for him: Salai, or "Little Devil."

The artist took the boy on as a servant or errand-boy but with an eye towards training him to be an artist — if he showed any talent, that is. About the only talent he did show those early months with Leonardo was the ability to get into trouble. The great artist took the time to write a list of all the mischief Salai caused in his studio, including stealing money from Leonardo's purse, snatching a pen from another apprentice, and generally raising hell of all sorts. Leonardo sums up the behavior of Salai with the words "thief, liar, obstinate, greedy."

---

85. Nicholl, Charles. *Leonardo Da Vinci: Flights of the Mind*. New York, NY: Penguin, 2005. Print, 250.

And Leonardo loved him.

Salai was a little Leonardo in his own right — or at least the little embodiment of the great artist's mischievousness. Like Tommaso, Salai would remain a fixture of Leonardo's life for decades to come.[86]

Don't Just Take my Word for It!

Here is one of Leonardo's entries in his notebook about the little devil Salai:

"The day after this I went to supper . . . and the aforesaid Giacomo [Salai] ate for two, and did mischief for four in so far as he broke three table-flasks and knocked over the wine."

As he finished establishing his new studio, wrapped up his work on Cecilia Gallerani's portrait, and grappled with the issues of designing the Sforza horse, Leonardo's already busy mind once again turned to pursuits other than his work. Like one of those intricate machines with innumerable cogs and wheels he was so fond of drawing in his notebooks, Leonardo's mind whirred with new ideas.

INTERLUDE: THE VITRUVIAN MAN

Ever since he was an apprentice in Andrea Verrocchio's studio back in Florence, Leonardo had been fascinated with human anatomy. In those early years, his study of the human form arose out of his dedication to painting realistic figures in his work — a skill that he revolutionized over his career. But starting in the late 1480s, Leonardo turned his formidable mind to issues that, up to then, had never been considered. You have to understand

---

86. Ibid. 271-272.

that in the world Leonardo inhabited, science itself remained a relic of the ancient past. Men like Galen, Hippocrates, and Aristotle had made important developments in medicine — but that was over 1,000 years before Leonardo was born. Scientific inquiry had basically stopped with the fall of the Roman Empire, only to be picked up recently in the 1400s.

By the time Leonardo turned his mind to the subject, human anatomy was even more shrouded in mystery than other scientific fields. Many Christians felt that the human form should remain in the dark. Man, after all, was made in God's image and should not be stripped down to its parts like some sort of machine. And yet, that is precisely what Leonardo wanted to do.

The great artist-turned scientist made diagrammatic drawings of the human skull, the circulatory system, and countless other aspects of our anatomy.

The same year he entered the Corte Vecchia, Leonardo began compiling a systematic record of the measurements of a number of young men. He proceeded to record their measurements — from the tips of the toes to the top of their heads — and eventually arrived at a complete understanding of the proportions of the human body.

What developed from these studies has since become an iconic image of Leonardo's great mind: the *Vitruvian Man*. Named after Vitruvius, the Roman architect who first studied human proportion in relation to such geometric forms as the circle and square, Leonardo drew the *Vitruvian Man* to illustrate the proportions of the human figure.[87]

---

87. Zöllner, Frank et. al. *Leonardo da Vinci: The Complete Paintings*. Köln: Taschen, 2011. Print, 106.

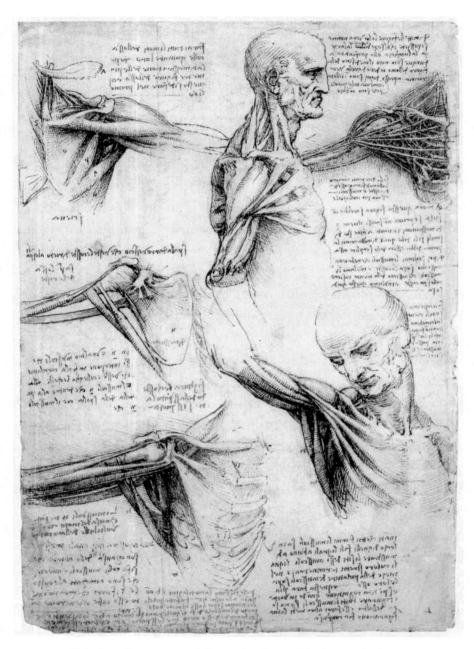

Sketches of anatomy and the mechanisms of the human body are
spread throughout Leonardo's notebooks — {{PD-1923}}

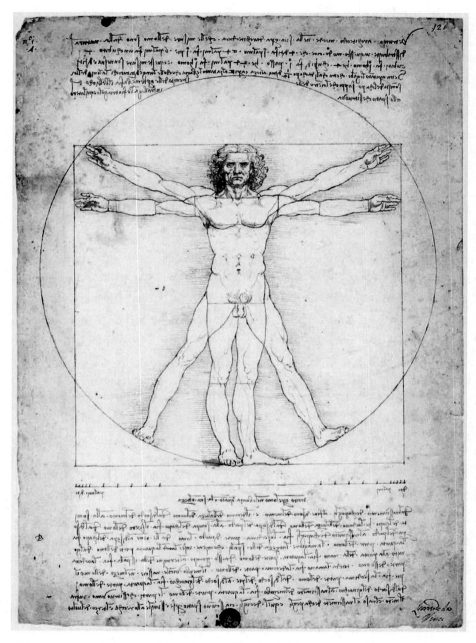

Vitruvian Man, Leonardo da Vinci, c. 1487; one of the most recognizable examples of Leonardo's studies of human anatomy and proportions — {{PD-1923}}

It seems odd to us today that at the very moment he realized his goal of getting the commission for the horse, Leonardo immediately turned his attention away from it towards something as strange as human anatomy. It's true that Leonardo had had similar moments of Attention Deficit Disorder-like sidetracks, but those were towards useful studies like engineering. Granted, he didn't produce much as an engineer, but at least his knowledge of the field had helped in his relationship with Ludovico. What on earth did he hope to obtain by studying anatomy?

Well, it helps to understand that for Leonardo, knowledge was inherently good. Regardless of the purpose of that knowledge, Leonardo felt that humans should strive towards understanding. He would later write in one of his notebooks that "the acquisition of any knowledge whatever is always useful to the intellect, because it will be able to banish the useless things and retain those that are good. For nothing can be either loved or hated unless it is first known." Leonardo's search for insight into the human form was therefore just another side of his thirst for knowledge — a thirst that by his own admission was unquenchable.[88]

COMPLETING THE SFORZA HORSE: ALMOST

No matter how beneficial his search for knowledge was, Leonardo's study of the human form did not pay the bills. His *Vitruvian Man* was not the reason Ludovico invited him to live in the Corte Vecchia. Leonardo had a task to accomplish and with his redesigned plan in hand, he set out to build a life-sized model of the Sforza horse.

At the same time he was meticulously taking measurements of young men for his own interest in human anatomy, Leonardo spent much of his time

88. Suh, H. Anna., ed. *Leonardo's Notebooks: Writing and Art of the Great Master*. New York: Black Dog & Leventhal, 2005. Print, 392.

in the royal stables studying horses. If you remember, Leonardo had always had a passion for animals in general and horses in particular. When Ludovico opened his stables of thoroughbred horses to the artist, Leonardo jumped at the chance, eventually taking as meticulous of measurements of the horses as he did his human models. The end result was not only a more realistic model for the Sforza statue but a written book on horses.

Finally, after years of drawings, the near-disaster of losing the commission, and his redesign from the Pavia statue, Leonardo was ready to get to work. Over the course of several months, he slaved away in the high-ceilinged studio in the Corte Vecchia, taking tons of clay and molding it into a model. After fashioning the base and the striding horse, Leonardo had to move his model outside for more room. The horse alone was 21 feet tall, far too tall for even the grand courtroom of the Corte Vecchia.

After several more weeks of work, Leonardo finished. In November of 1493, the artist stood to the side of the colossal model, which was covered by an enormous heap of canvas waiting to be pulled off for the special unveiling. In a courtyard before the Castello Sforzesco the time had come. With a flourish, Leonardo's apprentices pulled the canvas away to reveal the product of their master's hard work.

The crowd stood in awe.

If Leonardo still had critics, they were permanently silenced by the colossus before them. The final model — base, horse and figure — measured nearly 50 feet tall and towered over the buildings that surrounded the courtyard.[89] Francesco Sforza, Ludovico's father, appeared in armor, sitting proudly atop a majestic horse. The meticulous detail that Leonardo took in his

---

89. Bramly, Serge. *Leonardo: The Artist and the Man*. London: Penguin, 1994. Print, 232-233.

studies of the animals bore fruit and the massive horse stood in the court-yard as if ready to charge forth and conquer Milan's enemies.

Don't Just Take my Word for It!

Baldassare Taccone, a court poet in Milan, wrote of Leonardo's model:

"See in the Corte how he [Ludovico] is having a great colossus made out of metal in memory of his father. I am certain that neither Greece nor Rome ever saw anything bigger. See how beautiful this horse is: Leonardo da Vinci alone has created it."

Ludovico, feeling happy that he had assigned this important commission to the relatively inexperienced sculptor Leonardo, gave the artist his blessing to begin casting the final statue in bronze. Leonardo was about to make his biggest mark yet in the world of Renaissance art. A bronze statue at the scale he had modelled would remain an icon for centuries to come. And all of this would have come to pass had fate not once again intervened, throwing Leonardo and the rest of Italy into turmoil.

War appeared once more on the horizon.

DREAMS MELT AWAY

At the height of his success in Milan, Leonardo's well-laid plans began to fall apart. Later in life, he would remark that pain and pleasure go hand-in-hand. "If you take pleasure know that he has behind him one who will deal Tribulation and Repentance."[90] Leonardo had spent the last several years

---

90. Suh, H. Anna., ed. *Leonardo's Notebooks: Writing and Art of the Great Master*. New York: Black Dog & Leventhal, 2005. Print, 153.

awash in the accolades of Ludovico and others who admired his skill and the depths of his wisdom.

Pain for Leonardo now came at the head of an invading French army.

The year after Leonardo had unveiled the model for the Sforza horse, King Ferrante of Naples died suddenly. Naples had long been an enemy to Ludovico, primarily because Ferrante's daughter was the wife of the real Duke of Milan, Ludovico's nephew Giangaleazzo. Frustrated over Ludovico's overreach of power, Naples agitated against him. Remember, Ludovico was just the regent to Giangaleazzo, the true Duke of Milan who was supposed to attain power when he became an adult, which he now had been for some time. Despite coming of age, Giangaleazzo wasn't able to take power away from his uncle, Ludovico. The Moor had become too entrenched in his position at the head of Milan.

With the death of King Ferrante came the French. For centuries, the kingdom of France had had its sight on the Kingdom of Naples. The death of Ferrante gave them the excuse they were looking for. King Charles VIII of France invaded Italy. The way to Italy from France ran through the territory of Milan. Preferring the French over King Ferrante's successor in Naples, Ludovico first allied himself with the invading army of Charles. The same year of the invasion, Giangaleazzo conveniently died, leaving Ludovico in sole power of Milan. Well, almost — the French liked Milan quite a bit and were thinking of taking it along with Naples and, while they were at it, the rest of Italy. A year after the invasion Ludovico switched sides and joined the anti-French alliance in defeating the French army at the Battle of Fornovo in July of 1495.[91]

---

91. Bartlett, Kenneth R. *A Short History of the Italian Renaissance*. Toronto: Toronto UP, 2013, Print, 184.

This wouldn't be the end of the French in the story of Leonardo da Vinci's life. But that's for another chapter.

Meanwhile, one of the early casualties of this new war was Leonardo's equestrian statue. Nearly 75 tons of bronze had been set aside for the final casting at an enormous expense to the city. Bronze, a metal produced by mixing copper and tin with smaller amounts of additional metals, was extremely expensive. Generally, the metal was only used for small items. It was also used, on a grander scale, for producing cannons.[92] Preferring cannons to fight off the French over a massive statue, Ludovico took back the bronze he had given to Leonardo for the horse. None was left for his statue and the coffers of Milan were quickly running dry.

The project Leonardo had spent over a decade maneuvering to get and working to complete now came to an abrupt end. There would be no equestrian statue.[93]

FROM THE ASHES: THE LAST SUPPER

We can imagine that Leonardo at first would have been dismayed as it dawned on him that he would never actualize his dream of completing the equestrian statue. But in reality, Leonardo had already achieved a great deal in just the lead up to the feat itself. Over the years of working to get the commission, he had achieved a name for himself as the finest painter in Milan and had gotten in the good graces of Ludovico. In the years he spent designing the actual statue, he had learned a great deal about horses and human proportions (thanks especially to his flights of fancy in human anatomy), and when he unveiled the scale model of the statue he gained almost as much acclaim as he would have had he finished it in bronze.

92. Nicholl, Charles. *Leonardo Da Vinci: Flights of the Mind*. New York, NY: Penguin, 2005. Print, 282.
93. Bramly, Serge. *Leonardo: The Artist and the Man*. London: Penguin, 1994. Print, 248.

At the end of it all, he was far better off than he had been nearly 15 years ago when he first entered the city as a musician. Still, for a creative mind like Leonardo's that had spent so long working towards a goal, losing the chance to complete the horse had to have pained him. Well over a year after the bronze had been taken away, Leonardo wrote to Ludovico about another project. At the end of the letter, the artist writes sadly "About the horse I will say nothing for I know what times these are." True, he had grown accustomed to not finishing projects — he was notorious for this actually — but this was a project he wanted to see completed.

Fate had other ideas, however. And yet, fate gave Leonardo a great gift just as it took the horse from him. The same year he realized his statue would never be completed, Leonardo was given a commission for what some could argue would be his most famous work ever: the mural of the *Last Supper*.

As part of his larger civic building projects, Ludovico had spent several years refinishing the church of Santa Maria delle Grazie, which lay to the west of the Castello Sforzesco in Milan. Ludovico hoped to one day be buried in the church and so lavished it with the best he could offer. Who better to paint a mural on a wall in the church dining room than his favorite painter, Leonardo da Vinci?

Therefore, in 1495 Leonardo began the project of painting a large biblical scene onto the wall. The scene in question would be of Jesus and his disciples as they broke bread for the final time before Jesus' crucifixion. It was a relatively popular moment in the Bible that other artists had depicted before. Leonardo, however, was no ordinary artist. He set about applying his unique talent to the time-honored scene. Past examples of the scene showed Jesus and the disciples in rather stiff, stock poses. Viewing the painting, you would recognize it only by what was depicted: a table stocked with wine and bread and Jesus surrounded by his disciples, including Judas — the man who would betray him.

Last Supper, Leonardo da Vinci, c. 1495 — {{PD-1923}}

Rather than depict the generic scene from scripture of breaking bread, Leonardo chose to show the very instant that Jesus revealed to his disciples that one among them would betray him. Over the course of the next two years, Leonardo and his host of assistants including Salai and Tommaso went to work on the nearly 30 foot-long and 15-foot tall mural. Leonardo's work on the masterpiece sums up the artist's personality and work style to perfection.

Writing later in life, the novelist Matteo Bandello remembered watching Leonardo paint the Last Supper:

"He would arrive early, climb up on to the scaffolding and set to work. Sometimes he stayed there from dawn to sunset, never once laying down his brush, forgetting to eat and drink, painting without pause. At other times he would go for two, three, or four days without touching his

brush, but spending several hours a day in front of the work, his arms folded, examining and criticizing the figures to himself. I also saw him, driven by some sudden urge, at midday, when the sun was at its height, leaving the Corte Vecchia . . . to come straight to Santa Maria dell Grazie, without seeking shade, and clamber up on to the scaffolding, pick up a brush, put in one or two strikes, and then go away again."[94]

Here was Leonardo the great artist: sometimes consumed by his work and forgetting all else around him, other times getting distracted by other projects and ignoring his painting until some urge drove him back to it. The prior at the church (the man in charge) became so frustrated with Leonardo's irregular schedule that he complained frequently to Ludovico. In response, Leonardo told the Duke that he was still searching for a face evil enough to represent Judas, but that if the prior insisted on rushing his work he "could always use the head of that tactless and impatient prior" as a model. Here was Leonardo the mischievous country boy, the man who loved people like Tommaso and Salai and who got along well with the rough-hewn Ludovico. For his part, the Moor laughed at Leonardo's response and ignored the prior.

Finally, around 1497 the mural was finished.

Leonardo had outdone himself. The same skill of depicting life-like emotion he had shown in his *Madonna of the Carnation* back in Florence, he had perfected in the *Last Supper*. You can see the sheer astonishment in the eyes of the disciples as Jesus tells them of the approaching betrayal. A commentator on the mural explains it best:

---

94. Nicholl, Charles. *Leonardo Da Vinci: Flights of the Mind*. New York, NY: Penguin, 2005. Print, 292.

"Through their deeds and gestures [in the mural], they seem to be speaking among themselves, one man to another and he to yet another, afflicted with keen sense of wonder. Thus worthily our Leonardo created it with his delicate hand."[95]

From the ashes of the lost equestrian statue, Leonardo had accomplished his greatest work to date. Yet, fate seemed poised to once more flip the coin from pleasure to pain for Leonardo. The French had returned again, and this time Ludovico wouldn't be clever enough to avoid disaster.

---

95. Ibid. 297.

CHAPTER 8

Leonardo on the Move

The French invaded Italy a second time in 1499. This time, King Louis XII led the force, his cousin King Charles VIII having since died. Remembering the double-crossing of Ludovico Sforza, King Louis entered Italy and immediately besieged the city of Milan, finally capturing the Castello Sforzesco shortly thereafter. Although he temporarily escaped his enemies, Ludovico, Leonardo da Vinci's patron of nearly 20 years, was finally captured by the French and sent to France as a prisoner. He died eight years later in France.[96]

Amid the struggle for power in Milan, Leonardo fled the city. He had stayed around long enough to greet the conquering army of King Louis and probably to meet the ruler himself. However, given the uncertainty of the situation (and the fate of his patron) Leonardo determined that his time had come to move to greener pastures. After nearly 20 years in the city, the artist — now 47 years old — set out with his group of apprentices and companions on what would be the start of a unique chapter in his career. The next seven years would be an important chance for Leonardo to tie up loose ends back in Florence and to push the boundaries of his own genius.

---

96. Bartlett, Kenneth R. *A Short History of the Italian Renaissance*. Toronto: Toronto UP, 2013, Print, 186.

THE LUXURY OF MANTUA AND THE CANALS OF VENICE

Leonardo didn't immediately return to Florence after setting out from Milan. There were some detours. The first stop on his journey was the town of Mantua, located to the east between Milan and Florence. Isabella d'Este ruled the city as the wife of Mantua's leader Francesco Gonzaga II. In her mid-20s, Isabella was a prima donna — a spoiled brat who enjoyed the glitter and show of the good life almost as much as she loved the attention that life brought her. She had met Leonardo when she visited Milan in 1491 and when he painted the beautiful portrait of Ludovico's mistress, Cecilia Gallerani, Isabella was the one who asked Cecilia to send her the portrait so she could marvel at its beauty.

Leonardo knew that he could find safe harbor in Isabella's court, giving him enough time to actually figure out what he wanted to do next. Over the winter of 1499-1500, the homeless artist enjoyed the hospitality of Isabella, who herself enjoyed having such a famous person under her roof. During the short few months he stayed in Mantua, Leonardo drew a fine portrait of Isabella. Although Isabella loved the drawing, Leonardo was chaffing under the demanding young woman's finger and he was eager to leave Mantua, which he finally did in spring of 1500.[97]

Dragging his entourage with him — which definitely included Salai and possibly Tommaso — Leonardo then traveled to the famous trading city of Venice, located on the Adriatic coast of eastern Italy. While in Venice, Leonardo resumed his by-then comfortable role of military engineer. Like his work in Milan, however, none of the ideas Leonardo devised while in Venice actually came to anything. He did have some fantastical ideas, though. Among them included a suit that a man could wear that would allow him to breathe underwater for a time (a diving suit).

---

97. Bramly, Serge. *Leonardo: The Artist and the Man.* London: Penguin, 1994. Print, 310.

Meanwhile, Leonardo learned that the French had captured his former patron, Ludovico. If Leonardo had been intending to return to Milan when Ludovico regained power, these hopes were now dashed. Although by now a famous artist, Leonardo now faced the world untethered to a base of power and support. He certainly could — and would soon — receive commissions from other patrons, but for the time being Leonardo was insecure in his income for the first time since he had entered Milan those many years ago. As many people do when facing trials and tribulations, Leonardo looked for comfort back home. Once more, he set out for the city of his youth.

HOMECOMING

By mid-April 1500 Leonardo da Vinci walked the streets of Florence once again. His time away had done wonders to his reputation. He had left in a cloud of uncertainty and now returned a famous artist much in demand — although lacking both a house and a patron. He found a house readily enough, not far from Andrea Verrocchio's old studio. Now dead, Andrea had given his studio to Leonardo's fellow apprentice and now colleague, Lorenzo di Credi.

Settling back into life in the familiar surroundings of Florence, Leonardo recognized one major difference: the Medici were nowhere to be seen. Lorenzo de'Medici had died in 1492, leaving the city in control of his incompetent son, Piero. Following Lorenzo's death, anti-Medici factions in the city ousted Piero de'Medici. After yet another violent coup in 1498, the city of Florence once more settled into a time of peace. For the first time in nearly a century, however, there were no leading men in charge, and Florence returned to a period of actual republican rule. When Leonardo came back to Florence, the Florentine Republic was happy for its prodigal son to return.[98]

Ser Piero da Vinci, on the other hand, was at best lukewarm to his son's return. Now in his mid-70s, Leonardo's father had no less than 11 legitimate children from four different marriages. The return of his illegitimate son only complicated things for the aging notary. If father and son had frequently written each other over the years, we only have a draft of one letter between them as evidence. Chances are, the somewhat tense relationship they had when Leonardo left remained when he returned. But Leonardo soon found he didn't have much time to worry about it. Now a famous artist, he quickly acquired a load of commissions from newfound admirers. In a few years' time, he would regret not spending time with his father while he had the chance.

FAME IN FLORENCE

Within a short time, Leonardo had moved into the Church of Santissima Annunziata, where the friars there had commissioned the artist to paint an altarpiece for their chapel. The last time he had been commissioned to paint for a church in Florence, he left the work unfinished at the church of San Donato at Scopeto. The terms for that commission were horrible for the artist, who would have been paid 150 florins only after the work was completed. This time, however, the friars at the church of Santissima Annunziata were paying for Leonardo's living expenses and those of his household in addition to an unknown amount of cash money.

18 years had made all the difference.

---

98. Bartlett, Kenneth R. *A Short History of the Italian Renaissance*. Toronto: Toronto UP, 2013, Print, 239-240.

But, Leonardo was still Leonardo and he left the friars waiting quite a while before even beginning the painting. This time, however, his clients were willing to wait without complaint. After all, this was Leonardo da Vinci who was painting it! The more fame an artist had, the more a client was willing to live with his eccentricities. Finally, however, Leonardo unveiled the drawing of the painting, which featured St. Anne, the infant Jesus and the Virgin Mary. Much like the fanfare around his unveiling of the clay model of the equestrian statue, this unveiling in the church attracted large crowds of onlookers.[99]

Don't Just Take my Word for It!

Giorgio Vasari, Leonardo's early biographer describes the unveiling:

> *"This work not only won the astonished admiration of all the artists, but when it was finished for two days it attracted to the room where it was exhibited a crowd of men and women, young and old, who flocked there as if they were attending a great festival, to gaze in amazement at the marvels he had created."*[100]

Just as he had done his entire career, Leonardo had taken so long to complete the drawing for the friars because he was distracted with other odd jobs. For instance, in early 1501 Leonardo left Florence entirely for a brief trip to Rome. The disappointment of 20 years ago when Lorenzo de'Medici had overlooked him to paint the Sistine Chapel was still fresh in Leonardo's mind. Instead of arriving to paint a famous commission, this time Leonardo apparently travelled as a simple tourist. He studied the ancient ruins around the city and spent time expanding his knowledge of engineering.

---

99. Nicholl, Charles. *Leonardo Da Vinci: Flights of the Mind*. New York, NY: Penguin, 2005. Print, 332.
100. Vasari, Giorgio. *The Lives of the Artists*. Trans. Julia C. Bondanella and Peter Bondanella. New York: Oxford UP, 1991. Print, 293.

Finally, after just a few months, Leonardo returned to Florence in time to put the finishing touches on the drawing for the friars and unveil the work-in-progress for all to admire.[101]

"OUR MOST EXCELLENT AND WELL-BELOVED ARCHITECT AND GENERAL ENGINEER LEONARDO"

In just over a year's time, Leonardo had travelled from Milan to Mantua, to Venice to Florence to Rome and back to Florence. 18 years in one city had given the aging artist a thirst for travel. When he returned from his educational trip to Rome in the spring of 1501, he spent the rest of the year much as he had the previous one: following every whim of his mind and accomplishing very little (including making no more headway on the painting for the friars). For several months he had also been dodging the persistent requests from Isabella d'Este for him to paint a portrait of her.

Apparently, however, just as he had done back in Milan after the portrait of Cecilia Gallerani, Leonardo had once again tired of the paint brush. His mind had turned away from painting. Writing to Isabella from Florence, the churchman Fra Pietro Novellara tells the impatient lady that Leonardo's "mathematical [engineering] experiments have distracted him so much from painting that he cannot abide the paintbrush."

If nothing else, Leonardo's mind was constantly seeking new sources of inspiration and interest. Painting had grown stale to the artist. This strange mixture of restlessness and loss of interest in painting drove Leonardo into the arms of Cesare Borgia. The son of the current pope in Rome, Cesare was an enterprising man of growing power. On an incessant mission to gain more control, Cesare had taken mercenary troops and carved out his

---

101. Nicholl, Charles. *Leonardo Da Vinci: Flights of the Mind*. New York, NY: Penguin, 2005. Print, 335.

own kingdom in the central region of Italy, just north of Rome.[102] All of this land-grabbing frightened the leaders of Florence and nearby city-states. Hoping to build a diplomatic bridge between Florence and this young prince, Florence sent Leonardo da Vinci to him in the summer of 1502. It is likely Florence hoped Leonardo would be the same type of artist-diplomat the Medici used to employ when they were in power.

Leonardo had met Cesare in 1499 during the brief time the artist remained in Milan while the French were in the city. Cesare had traveled to Milan and helped the French army during their conquest of the region. For this support, France lent Cesare their support and a sizable army of soldiers. Leonardo and Cesare must have taken an instant liking to each other. From Cammelli the poet, to Tommaso the magician-prankster to the tough-guy Ludovico Sforza, Leonardo always gravitated towards independent-minded men. Cesare Borgia was certainly that. For his part, Cesare must have liked Leonardo's intelligence, his creativity and humor. Now, three years later, Leonardo set out from Florence to meet up once again with this active young ruler.

He took a roundabout route to reach Cesare in his stronghold of Urbino. The purpose of the many sidetracks was to study the fortifications and buildings of Cesare's new dominion. You see, Florence hadn't just sent Leonardo as a diplomat, but to be Cesare's military engineer and general architect. Unlike his time as an engineer under Ludovico Sforza, however, Leonardo would actually provide a much needed service to his new employer. Cesare was on an active military campaign, traveling from one city to another. He needed assistance in matters of building and defeating fortifications. That's where Leonardo da Vinci would fit in.

---

102. Chambers, David. *Popes, Cardinals and War: the Church Militant in Early Modern and Renaissance Europe.* Tauris, 2006. Print, 98-99.

From Florence, Leonardo went to the coastal town of Piombino where he studied the small town's walls and fortified towers. From there, he struck inland to the city of Arezzo and through the Apennine Mountains along the spine of Italy. There Leonardo studied the topography. From these calculations and sketches, he made detailed maps of the area for Cesare, the better for him to move his armies where they were needed. Finally Leonardo reached Urbino, a walled town on a hill along the eastern shores of Italy. He didn't remain long in the town. Neither did Cesare. Having only recently conquered the towns of central Italy, Cesare Borgia constantly had to stamp out one rebellion after another. He lived on the campaign trail as much as in his fortresses.[103]

Over the next three weeks, Leonardo kept track of his many travels in one of his notebooks. Each stop he made, the enthusiastic engineer took the time to sketch and take measurements of an interesting bridge. Or he would peruse a local library or otherwise study something he hadn't seen before. If he had grown tired of painting and sitting idly in Florence, Leonardo was now getting his fill of new sights and experiences. In August of that year, Cesare wrote up a passport for Leonardo so that the architect/engineer and his retinue could travel freely through the war-zone of central Italy. In the document, Cesare ordered his troops to allow Leonardo passage through his entire kingdom and to lend Leonardo any assistance he may need. Leonardo da Vinci was, after all, "our most excellent and well-beloved architect and general engineer."[104]

Leonardo wasn't just an engineer on paper, either. He spent the rest of that year marching with Cesare's armies and helping build and redesign fortifications throughout the area. In one particular instance, he designed and built a huge bridge for Cesare's army to cross a wide river that was block-

103. Nicholl, Charles. *Leonardo Da Vinci: Flights of the Mind*. New York, NY: Penguin, 2005. Print, 345.
104. Bramly, Serge. *Leonardo: The Artist and the Man*. London: Penguin, 1994. Print, 325.

ing their advance. For really the first time in his life, Leonardo built in the real world what he had been studying and theorizing about for decades. Of course, we can assume he had done some building during his time in Milan, but never on the scale he now experienced. His new life on the road was a strenuous, but practical, one. For Leonardo, that was enough for now.

His time as a military engineer came to an end, however, during the winter of 1502-1503. We don't know what caused him to leave his employ with Cesare, but following a particularly brutal squashing of another rebellion, the two men split ways. Perhaps the aging Leonardo had had enough of life on the military campaign. He would later write that war "is the most brutal kind of madness there is." Leonardo had thirsted for a life of activity and practical engineering. He had gotten his fill and then some.

MONA LISA

In March of 1503, Leonardo da Vinci entered Florence yet again, this time to return to the world of a famous painter. This, then, was the context for what most would consider Leonardo's greatest painting: the enigmatic, yet beautiful *Mona Lisa*. Fortunately, we know quite a bit about the commission of the painting. Lisa del Giocondo was born in 1479 to the respectable Florentine Antonmaria Gherardini. In 1495, the young Lisa married Francesco del Giocondo, a well-to-do businessman who came from a family of silk merchants. Francesco had held civic offices and counted as associates some very important families in Florence. In April of 1503, Francesco moved his wife and their three children to a new home in the city. With walls to fill, Francesco sought the skill of the famed Leonardo da Vinci to paint a portrait of his wife, Lisa.

Mona Lisa, Leonardo da Vinci, 1510; arguably Leonardo's most famous painting, the portrait is of Francesco del Giocondo's wife, Lisa — {{PD-1923}}

Fun Fact

"Mona" was a polite form of address, a lot like our "Ma'am" or "Miss." So, the *Mona Lisa* basically means *Miss Lisa*.

In typical Leonardian fashion, however, the painting would never hang in the client's house. Leonardo wouldn't finish the painting until 1510 or sometime later, by which time he no longer lived in Florence. That's right, what is arguably the most famous painting in the world, Leonardo's masterpiece, never reached its intended owner.[105] Despite the fame the painting now has, it received only minor attention during Leonardo's lifetime. His famous biographer, Giorgio Vasari only gives one sentence to the painting in his lengthy praise of Leonardo's life and work. There is no doubt, however, that the expert control of light and shadow, his fine detail to shades of color and the positioning of his subject, mark Leonardo's *Mona Lisa* as a stunning achievement.

Fun Fact

The *Mona Lisa* entered the public eye when it was stolen from the Louvre museum in 1911. The culprit was a 33-year-old Italian painter-decorator, Vicenzo Peruggia. He had worked for a time at the Louvre, which was how he was able to enter the museum unchallenged and exit it again with the painting hidden inside his jacket. Vicenzo was a patriotic Italian who fervently believed that Leonardo's most famous portrait should be displayed in an Italian museum.

---

105. Zöllner, Frank et. al. *Leonardo da Vinci: The Complete Paintings*. Köln: Taschen, 2011. Print. 160.

After keeping the painting hidden in a chest in his room for two years, Vicenzo got caught trying to sell the portrait to the Uffizi Gallery in Florence. *Mona Lisa* had been stolen from the Louvre as a rather unknown painting, but she returned a world-famous one.[106]

DUELING PAINTERS: LEONARDO AND MICHELANGELO

The *Mona Lisa* was not the only painting Leonardo left unfinished during his brief return to Florence. The artist never painted that stunning drawing for the friars at the church of Santissima Annunziata — apparently his travels with Cesare Borgia had interfered, and he never picked the project back up when he returned. Still working on the *Mona Lisa*, Leonardo took on yet another painting commission in 1503. Like all the others he had started since arriving in Florence in 1500, Leonardo would leave this painting unfinished as well. Unlike the other ones, however, Leonardo might have actually had a good reason to leave it half-done.

The commission had come from the Florentine Signoria, which asked Leonardo to paint a massive painting on a wall in the Grand Council Chamber of the Palazzo Vecchio. The scene the Signoria wanted depicted was the climactic *Battle of Anghiari*, which took place in 1440 when the Florentine forces defeated their Milanese opponents during one of the many wars between the two cities.

The large composition was intended to be one of two such paintings. The other, located next to the space Leonardo was to paint his scene, was going to depict another famous battle in Florence's recent history. The artist the Signoria chose to paint this competing scene was the new, up-and-coming painter Michelangelo Buonarroti.

---

106. Nicholl, Charles. *Leonardo Da Vinci: Flights of the Mind*. New York, NY: Penguin, 2005. Print, 369.

Battle of Anghiari, Leonardo da Vinci; in typical Leonardo style, the painting was left unfinished, abandoned in favor of more interesting pursuits — {{PD-1923}}

Nearly half the age of Leonardo, Michelangelo represented the new wave of artists who arose during Leonardo's 18-year absence from the city. Michelangelo had grown up hearing about Leonardo's exploits in Milan and certainly sought to challenge Leonardo's title as Florence's best painter. The Signoria no doubt anticipated the two artists' rivalry with each other (after all, the more competition, the better the two paintings should be). Unfortunately, all it did was cause antagonism. To Leonardo, Michelangelo was brash, inexperienced and aggressively self-confident. To Michelangelo, Leonardo was old, too set in his ways and not all that great of an artist to begin with. Each man disliked the other in equal measure.

Their dislike of each other sometimes spilled over into the public view. One day while walking the streets of Florence, Leonardo passed by a group of men who were arguing over a passage in a famous book when the group called the artist over to give them his opinion. Just then, Michelangelo passed by and Leonardo said, "There's Michelangelo, he'll explain it for you." Michelangelo, thinking Leonardo was trying to embarrass him, retorted, "Explain it yourself — you who designed a horse to cast in bronze, and couldn't cast it, and abandoned it out of shame." The horse Michelangelo was referencing, of course, was the Sforza horse statue, likely still a sore spot for Leonardo.[107]

Despite the uncomfortable atmosphere, Leonardo began laying out the *Battle of Anghiari* painting. For the rest of that year and the beginning of the next, he and his pupils worked on the design until spring of 1504 when he started the painting itself. Fate would not allow the great artist much time on the painting, however. On July 9, 1504 Leonardo's father died.

Death and a Homecoming

> *"On Wednesday at the 7th hour Ser Piero da Vinci died, on the 9th day of July 1504."*

These are the few words Leonardo writes regarding his father's death. Ser Piero left nothing to his illegitimate son, Leonardo. Instead, all his money and possessions went to his 11 legitimate children. Although it probably didn't come as a surprise to Leonardo, nevertheless it had to have stung. A few weeks later, Leonardo left Florence for a brief trip back to Vinci. By now, his mother Caterina had been dead for an unknown number of years, her passing going unremarked by Leonardo. Perhaps spurred on by his fa-

---

107. Ibid. 379.

ther's death, Leonardo returned to Vinci to visit the one man who had been more a father figure to him than his own father: his uncle, Francesco.

Back in 1492 Francesco, who was childless, had created a will in agreement with Ser Piero. In this 1492 will, Francesco's possessions would go to Ser Piero's 11 legitimate children. However, after learning that Ser Piero completely ignored Leonardo in his own will, Francesco changed his mind. When Leonardo visited him in August of 1504, Francesco wrote up a new will — this one giving all his possessions to Leonardo, who he loved like the son he never had.

Leonardo stayed for a time in Vinci, enjoying the temporary escape from Florence. In Florence sat his unfinished work, which had begun to pile up, and that irritating Michelangelo, always ready with an insult. Florence also now contained the ghost of his father. Given these burdens waiting for him back in the city, it's understandable that Leonardo used this opportunity for a little vacation. After leaving Vinci, he traveled to some coastal towns where he sketched buildings and generally distracted himself from the death of his father and his other worries. Finally, recognizing that his problems wouldn't just disappear, he returned to Florence at the end of 1504.[108]

THINKING OF FLIGHT

Immediately after returning from his brief vacation, Leonardo threw himself into his work, painting tirelessly in the Palazzo Vecchio and on the *Mona Lisa*. He gathered his apprentices and assistants and set them to work as well. Tommaso returned to Leonardo's side at this time and helped the artist by mixing paints. For the next several months, Leonardo worked on the *Battle of Anghiari*. However, between his general feeling of depression and a series of unfortunate mistakes, the painting was not coming together

---

108. Ibid. 388.

as quickly as the Signoria wanted.[109] By June of 1505, the Florentine officials were growing tired of his delays and Leonardo grew tired of the Florentine officials. When they tried to pay him for some of his supplies in small coins, Leonardo exploded, saying, "I am no penny painter!"[110] The relationship between the painter and patron began to deteriorate rapidly.

As he had done in Milan during times of plague and despair, Leonardo escaped from his external problems in Florence by retreating within himself. He spent less and less time on his paintings and more time thinking about a pet project he had put aside almost 20 years ago: the idea of human flight. After years of studying the flight of birds, Leonardo had identified what he thought was the secret. Back in Milan he had designed a parachute, which would allow a man to float safely down from towering heights. This time, Leonardo wanted a machine that could propel a man through the air like a bird. His sketches show a variety of possible flying machines, none of them very feasible in reality. The one that looks closest to a modern air glider might have allowed a man to glide through the air, but not to propel himself.

It is likely this machine that Leonardo (or one of his assistants) tested in early 1505. In one of his notebooks, Leonardo excitedly exclaims, "the big bird will take its first flight above the back of the Great Cecero [Mt. Ceceri outside of Florence], filling the universe with amazement, filling all the chronicles with its fame, and bringing eternal glory to the nest where it was born." Unfortunately, the "big bird" did none of those things. We can assume no one died in the attempt, since none of the familiar sources mention anything like that. The machine probably just fell apart before it could even gain altitude.[111]

109. Bramly, Serge. *Leonardo: Artist and the Man*. London: Penguin, 1994. Print, 347.
110. Nicholl, Charles. *Leonardo Da Vinci: Flights of the Mind*. New York, NY: Penguin, 2005. Print, 379.
111. Ibid. 395.

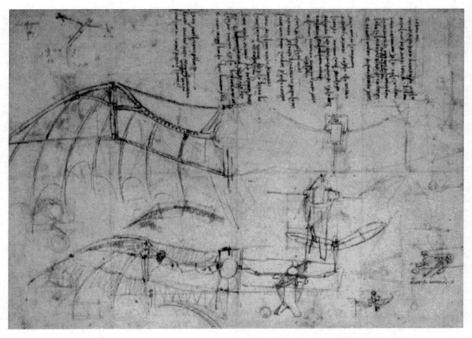

Notebook sketch of the 'big bird' glider machine that Leonardo futilely hoped would bring the power of flight to mankind — {{PD-1923}}

His failed flight only made him more restless and frustrated with his work. He had returned to Florence hoping that his home city would give him a chance for a similar life he had enjoyed in Milan. Frustrated early on, he had escaped to the chaotic but blessedly active life of a military engineer. But he had burned out on that. Then he had thrown himself into a set of new paintings. But the death of his father and the antagonism with Michelangelo — and his own inherent restlessness — kept undermining him. In the beginning of 1506, Leonardo came to the realization that Florence had nothing for him now. Like he had done over 20 years before, Leonardo da Vinci prepared to leave the city of his youth.

CHAPTER 9

Leonardo and the French

Unhappy with his work by early 1506, Leonardo cast his eyes once more beyond the walls of Florence, looking for a way out. He didn't have to look for long.

A painting from Leonardo's past rescued him from his current dilemma. If you remember, Leonardo and Ambrogio de Predis had finished the *Virgin of the Rocks* altarpiece for a Milanese fraternity back in the 1480s. When they received the finished piece, the fraternity displayed the beautiful painting in the Church of San Francisco Grande in Milan. Then trouble arose. Leonardo and Ambrogio took stock of all the money and time they had put into the altarpiece and then at the paltry 800 lire the fraternity had paid them. They hadn't even broken even. Leonardo and Ambrogio submitted a formal complaint with Ludovico Sforza, claiming the fraternity had cheated them. The fraternity then responded by offering the two discontents 100 lire more for their troubles. Eventually, Ludovico agreed to buy the original painting from the fraternity, with the understanding that Ambrogio and Leonardo would then paint a substitute copy for display in the church.

By this time, Leonardo's restless attention had already turned away to something new: the equestrian statue commission for Ludovico. Ambrogio de Predis, on the other hand, couldn't afford to let the matter go. For the next several years, Ambrogio painted the copy altarpiece largely on his own, finally delivering it to the fraternity in 1499. But, Ambrogio couldn't pull a fast one on the fraternity, and they recognized that Leonardo had barely touched the painting. They refused to pay Ambrogio for the piece.

And so, the matter once more returned to the courts; this time the French had to deal with it.[112]

In 1506, the issue finally came to a head. The French agreed with the Fraternity that the painting hadn't been completed with enough Leonardian flair and was therefore "incomplete." If Leonardo and Ambrogio wanted to be paid, Leonardo would have to return to complete a new substitute copy.

Leonardo didn't complain.

When he left Florence for the first time in 1482, he left unfinished his *Saint Jerome* (the painting that the uncle of Napoleon Bonaparte would find scattered throughout the city three centuries later) as well as the painting for the church of San Donato at Scopeto. Now with the convenient excuse of needing to go back to Milan for a legal dispute, Leonardo left the city again in May of 1506. Just as before, the artist left Florence with several projects half-finished: the *Battle of Anghiari* fresco for the Signoria of Florence and the *Mona Lisa*. The fresco he would leave behind and forget about, but the half-finished *Mona Lisa* Leonardo took with him on his trip, hoping to finish it later.

This didn't sit well with the rulers of Florence. Although they begrudgingly let their prized artist leave the city, the Signoria made Leonardo sign an agreement stating that under the threat of a hefty fine, he would return to Florence within three months. Leonardo had spent his entire professional

---

112. Nicholl, Charles. *Leonardo Da Vinci: Flights of the Mind*. New York, NY: Penguin, 2005. Print, 198-199.

career flaunting such agreements, finishing or not finishing paintings on a whim. Why the Signoria actually thought he would stay true to this one remains a mystery. But with agreement in hand — a contract that meant less to Leonardo than the paper it was written on — the Signoria bade farewell to Leonardo da Vinci, possibly for the last time.

OUI OUI, MON AMI

In 1482 Leonardo had entered Milan an unknown young artist, clutching a resume he had mostly made up and a silver instrument he would rarely play. This time, he marched through the gates of St. Ambrose puffed up with the self-knowledge of an artist who knew his worth. The French in Milan welcomed him home with open arms. Back in 1499, Leonardo had greeted the conquering French army with one hand while seeking the nearest exit with the other. After all Ludovico Sforza, his patron of many years, had been evicted from the city, his fate at that time still unknown. Despite this cautious approach, Leonardo had taken an instant liking to the conquerors. When he had finally settled down again in Florence in 1501 (just before his brief foray as a military engineer with Cesare Borgia), Leonardo took a commission from Florimond Robertet, a favorite minister of King Louis of France. Robertet cherished the resulting painting, now called the *Madonna with a Yarn-Winder*, and proudly showed it to all he met, including the king. This painting, more than anything else, became the reason why the French so happily welcomed Leonardo to Milan in 1506.

Don't Just Take my Word for It!

The French King Louis XII loved Leonardo's work so much that when he first beheld the *Last Supper*, he wanted to take the painting back to France with him. Giorgio Vasari explains the scene:

> *"[the King wished] to take it back to his kingdom. As a result, he tried every method to find architects who might be able to protect it with beams of wood and iron so that it could safely be carried away, never considering the expense he might incur, so intensely did he wish to have it. But since the painting was done on a wall, His Majesty had to endure his longing for the work, and it was left to the Milanese.*[113]

When Charles d'Amboise, the new French governor of Milan, took over operations in the city, he was all too happy to use the dispute over the *Virgin of the Rocks* to pull Leonardo da Vinci back into the orbit of France. Leonardo didn't need much convincing and he immediately took up residence in the castle of the governor and began to enjoy the settled life of a Renaissance artist once again. If he hadn't already acknowledged it when he first left Florence those many years ago, Leonardo now understood that the city of his youth was just that — a city that deserved to be remember fondly but that had no more to give to the now mature artist. Milan, first under Ludovico Sforza and now the French, freely gave Leonardo the space, money, and encouragement to pursue every fancy the man developed. Milan had always been more his home than Florence.

Leonardo was soon reminded of this fact as he fell under the patronage of Charles d'Amboise. A young French nobleman who notoriously enjoyed all the fruits life offered — sometimes too freely — Charles admired Leonardo tremendously. When the three months had passed (during which time he

---

113. Vasari, Giorgio. *The Lives of the Artists*. Trans. Julia C. Bondanella and Peter Bondanella. New York: Oxford UP, 1991. Print, 291.

was supposed to settle the dispute over the painting), Leonardo nevertheless remained in Milan. Charles wrote the Florentine Signoria, requesting that they allow Leonardo to remain for a while longer. In reply, the Signoria wrote an angry letter to Charles. They demanded the return of their artist, as if Leonardo were a patented commodity that belonged to Florence.

Leonardo shrugged his shoulders and didn't give the matter a second thought. Rather than binding him to a single commission, the French in Milan treated the aging master (Leonardo by this time was already 54 years old) like a respected consultant. They went to him for all manner of advice — from designs for a new country garden and church to personal portraits or drawings. Leonardo was a hot commodity, constantly surrounded by people who respected his many talents. For the first time since leaving Milan seven years ago — aside from the brief experience with Cesare Borgia as a practicing engineer — people recognized Leonardo for more than his painting.

Don't Just Take my Word for It!

Writing in December of 1506, Charles tells the Signoria of Florence just what sort of a treasure Leonardo was to them:

> *"The excellent works accomplished in Italy and especially in Milan by Master Leonardo da Vinci, your fellow citizen, have made all those who see them singularly love their author, even if they have never met him . . . For ourselves, we confess that we loved him before meeting him personally. But now that we have been in his company and can speak from experience of his varied talents, we see in truth that his name, already famous for painting, remains comparatively unknown when on thinks of the praises he merits for the other gifts he possess, which are of extraordinary power."[114]*

114. Bramly, Serge. *Leonardo: The Artist and the Man*. London: Penguin, 1994. Print, 355.

This sounds almost like a backhanded accusation. After all, the very people who overlooked those "other gifts" of Leonardo, and who seemed to have undervalued him time and again were his "fellow citizens" of Florence. Most of the work Leonardo would later be known for — the *Vitruvian Man*, the *Last Supper* and even the *Mona Lisa* — were all the products of his time in Milan. If Florence had nurtured the boy, Milan had nurtured the artist and created the great Renaissance icon of Leonardo da Vinci.

There was no way the French were going to give Leonardo back to the very people who so mistreated him. When Florence continued to press the issue, King Charles himself stepped in. The king made it clear that continued good relations between France and Florence depended on Leonardo remaining in Milan.[115] Biting back their frustration, the Signoria agreed to let the matter drop and relinquished their claim on Leonardo.

BAD BLOOD

Despite this odd tug-of-war and his desire to remain in Milan, Leonardo returned to Florence in the summer of 1507. He had no intention whatsoever to return to the *Anghiari* fresco. The only reason he came back was to bury his uncle, Francesco, who had died. And to fight for his rightful inheritance, which Francesco had promised him three years earlier. Apparently not content with the entire estate of Piero da Vinci, Leonardo's half-siblings challenged Francesco's will giving large portions of land and money to the bastard-born artist. The French once more rallied to their "dear and well-beloved" Leonardo (that's what King Louis had begun calling him), and official letters from Milan and France clogged the inboxes of the Florentine courts.

---

115. Nicholl, Charles. *Leonardo Da Vinci: Flights of the Mind*. New York, NY: Penguin, 2005. Print, 408.

Despite this royal favor, the courts of Florence moved at an excruciatingly slow pace and Leonardo found himself sitting idly in Florence awaiting a decision. Well, not idly. This was Leonardo da Vici, after all. When he arrived in Florence to first deal with the dispute, Leonardo along with Salai, took up residence in the house of a rich patron of the arts. Piero di Braccio Martelli was an accomplished mathematician in his own right and freely gave his money and home to artists of all sorts, including now Leonardo. Also lodging in the household was Giovan Francesco Rustici, a graduate of Andrea Verrochio's studio many years after Leonardo himself had left. Rustici was eccentric, prone to moving from one project to another and had a coarse sense of humor. Leonardo got along splendidly with him.

Fun Fact

The studio the 30-year-old Rustici kept looked more like Noah's Ark than an artist's workspace. Rustici kept an eagle, a crow (who could speak like a man), a variety of snakes and a porcupine as tame as a pet dog. [116]

While waiting for the court's decision on his inheritance, Leonardo studied mathematics with Piero and anatomy with Rustici. He also took this opportunity to reorganize his notebooks, which by 1507 had accumulated in heaps of random papers. Meanwhile, the French grew impatient with the delay. Leonardo wrote back to Milan in early 1508 that he had reason to believe the case would be settled by Easter of that year. His intuition spot on, the Florentine courts soon returned with a verdict. They ruled in favor of Leonardo.

---

116. Bramly, Serge. *Leonardo: The Artist and the Man*. London: Penguin, 1994. Print, 357.

Having been cheated out of his father's inheritance, Leonardo now received some of Francesco's land around Vinci as well as a sum of money. He didn't need either, but Leonardo had pursued this case more as a matter of principle than out of hope of receiving anything in return.[117] From the moment he was born, Leonardo had inhabited a shadowy space between two worlds — the world of legitimacy and the love of two faithful parents and the world where bastards lived, ignored and treated as outcasts. He had never fully lived in either world, instead making his own way in life. He found support along the way — an understanding and loving uncle, a stern but compassionate tutor, and wacky, strange friends in every city he lived. The friendships he chose, the business relationships he entered into, and the art and knowledge he cultivated gave Leonardo a fulfilling life. With his uncle dead and the court ruling in his favor, Leonardo set out from Florence unburdened by the specter of both worlds, free to continue life in the world he himself had created.

BACK IN MILAN: OUT WITH THE OLD AND IN WITH THE NEW

Now back in the city of his choosing, Leonardo opened a new studio near the Porta Orientale on the outskirts of Milan. Once more, the master artist gathered together a household of apprentices, assistants, and Salai, the now grown young man who still acted like a "little devil." We don't know much about the other young men who worked with Leonardo at this time, except for one: Giovanni Francesco Melzi. Melzi soon became one part apprentice and one part secretary. Melzi's was the job of making appointments for the great artist, organizing his master's notebooks and otherwise ensuring the smooth operation of the studio.[118] More so than even Salai, Leonardo and

---

117. Ibid. 359.
118. Kemp, Martin. *Leonardo*. Oxford: Oxford UP, 2011. Print. 37. Nicholl, Charles. *Leonardo Da Vinci: Flights of the Mind*. New York, NY: Penguin, 2005. Print, 233.

Melzi became very close, and for the rest of the artist's life, the young Melzi would serve as his most trustworthy assistant and friend.

Fun Fact

15 years old when he met Leonardo, Giovanni Francesco Melzi came from a prominent family near Milan. His father, Girolamo, served the French as a captain in the army. As a gentleman coming from a well-to-do family, Francesco Melzi must have shocked his family when he told them he was going to follow Leonardo into the life of an artist. Strangely, they didn't protest at all. I guess if their son had to become an artist, at least he was training under the best Italy had to offer.[119]

Having settled his family affairs in Florence, Leonardo now wanted a fresh start. To get that, he had to free himself entirely of the projects that had dragged on this attention for the last several years. The first to go was the painting he had first envisioned as the altarpiece for the church of Santissima Annunziata in Florence. He took the drawings he had made for the cartoon — the one whose unveiling had attracted so many onlookers almost eight years before in Florence — and completed a large oil painting. Now known as the *Virgin and Child with St. Anne*, Leonardo would hold onto this piece for the rest of his life, perhaps waiting to sell it to an art-lover who could truly appreciate it (and pay for it).[120] Next, the master turned his attention to the *Mona Lisa*, adding the final touches to the now-famous portrait around 1510. Like the *Virgin and Child with St. Anne*, Leonardo held onto the *Mona Lisa* until his death.[121]

---

119. Bramly, Serge. *Leonardo: The Artist and the Man*. London: Penguin, 1994. Print, 169-170.

120. Zöllner, Frank et. al. *Leonardo da Vinci: The Complete Paintings*. Köln: Taschen, 2011. Print, 180.

121. Ibid. 155.

Of course, he wouldn't be Leonardo da Vinci if he focused his entire attention on just these paintings. While finishing old projects, Leonardo turned his attention to a topic that had intrigued him for years now: water. Over the course of six weeks in 1508, he wrote the book "Of the World and Its Waters," which explored the physics, the artistic depiction, and the general characteristics of water. The artist might have been inspired to study water because King Louis had just given him the water rights to a nearby canal in the Milanese countryside. The terms of this gift allowed Leonardo to sell excess water in the canal to nearby farmers — a revenue stream he would enjoy for the rest of his life.[122]

TRADING A PAINTBRUSH FOR A SCALPEL

As he added the final touches to the *Mona Lisa*, Leonardo's mind turned once more to the taboo subject of human anatomy. The studies he had made into the science back in the 1480s were taken up again with greater interest in 1508. We don't know exactly when Leonardo dissected his first human body, but his detailed drawings of the circulatory system back in the 1480s suggests he at least witnessed the procedure. Back then, however, the artist had been more interested in the mechanics of the body (its movement, appearance, etc.). Now, he sought to learn about the biology — the nitty gritty of life and death. When he had returned to Florence and was working on the *Battle of Anghiari*, Leonardo worked near the Santa Maria Novella hospital. He probably witnessed doctors dissecting deceased patients and might himself have taken up the scalpel a time or two. Now, back in Milan, he jumped fully into the field. At the end of 1508, Leonardo admitted to having dissected eight bodies.

Bodies weren't hard to find in Renaissance Milan.

---

122. Kemp, Martin. *Leonardo*. Oxford: Oxford UP, 2011. Print. 26.

Even without counting the plague, diseases of the day and lack of medical knowledge reduced the life expectancy to shocking lows. Those unfortunate people who died provided Leonardo with all the raw material he needed. He dissected the bodies of hanged men, old men who had died in hospitals, children and babies. As gruesome as the job may be, Leonardo's meticulous eye for detail uncovered a wealth of information never before recorded. He was the first person to ever notice the deterioration of arteries with age — a condition now known as arteriosclerosis. He delved into the study of human organs, their function and diseases that inflict them. He mapped the bones, bloody supply and muscles, literally laying bare the secrets of our bodies. All the while, he became more and more amazed at the subtle work of our existence, which he attributed to God, "who creates nothing superfluous or imperfect."[123]

By his own admission, between 1508 and 1517, Leonardo dissected around 30 bodies, filling his notebooks with sketches and musings on human form and function.[124]

CLOUDS ON THE HORIZON

In 1511, however, things started to go sour for Leonardo. That year, his great benefactor in the city — the governor Charles d'Amboise — died suddenly at a young age. Although his replacement from France continued to favor Leonardo, he wasn't as free with the king's money as Charles had been. These were the first echoes of thunder, the clouds gathering on the horizon bringing with them change in northern Italy. The peculiar nature of fate he had first recognized 20 years ago living in Milan, now rose to the surface of his mind once more. With pleasure, fate deals an equal measure of pain. Leonardo, at least, believed that and the events of the next two years seemed to confirm it.

123. Bramly, Serge. *Leonardo: The Artist and the Man*. London: Penguin, 1994. Print, 373.
124. Nicholl, Charles. *Leonardo Da Vinci: Flights of the Mind*. New York, NY: Penguin, 2005. Print, 444.

CHAPTER 10

Final Travels

Once again, Leonardo da Vinci's life fell victim to the unrelenting whims of higher powers. A man whose mind could pierce any barrier to human knowledge was nevertheless helpless in the face of marching armies and warring kingdoms. Facing France was an alliance of Italian city-states and the Holy Pope in Rome. Together, they formed "the Holy League." Already by the end of 1511, Swiss mercenaries employed by the Holy League were chipping away at French territories near Milan itself. On December 16 of that year, they razed the town of Desio, just 10 miles from Milan. From the city walls, Leonardo watched the orange glow illuminate the morning horizon and he drew the scene in one of his notebooks. In 1512, the big showdown between the French and the Italians took place near the city of Ravenna. At the end of the battle, the French governor of Milan lay dead. Although the French claimed victory, everyone else saw the writing on the wall.

Leonardo, who had escaped harm during the first French invasion of Milan more than a decade ago, took this time to go on an extended vacation in the countryside. Out among the vineyards and orchards, he would be far enough away from any dangers that might befall the French in the city of Milan. Leonardo took his household and his possessions to the country villa of his favorite assistant, Giovanni Francesco Melzi. Actually, the villa belonged to Melzi's father, who apparently didn't mind his house being invaded by an eccentric artist and his small army of assistants. We have no idea what Leonardo did for the entire year of 1512 — that whole year his notebooks sit silent. By the end of 1512, the French were finally expelled from Italy. Marching once more through the Ambrosian gates of Milan, a Sforza ascended to the head of the city. Not Ludovico, of course — he was several years dead by this point. His son, Massimiliano Sforza, however, proved a worthy successor to his father and on December 29, 1512 he re-established the family dynasty.[125]

During his period of seclusion in the rural hills of the Melzi villa, Leonardo da Vinci turned 60. Around this same time, he sat for his portrait to be drawn. The artist he trusted enough to capture his image for posterity? None other than Giovanni Francesco Melzi, who had only recently started his tutelage under the great master. The final drawing, executed in red chalk and ink depicts Leonardo in profile.

His long hair, which recedes slightly from his forehead, falls in waves about his shoulders. The most prominent feature of the portrait is his strong, equine nose. At 60-years-old, Leonardo looks alert, strong, and handsome.

Fun Fact

60 years old was old for the time. It is estimated that the majority of Italian artists died before they reached age 65. For the majority of the population who lived lives of less comfort, death came much sooner than that.[126]

125. Potter, David. *Renaissance France at War: Armies, Culture and Society, C.1480-1560.* Boydell Press, 2008. Print, 6-7.
126. McManus, I.C. "Life Expectation of Italian Renaissance Artists." *The Lancet*, Feb. 1, 1975, 266-267.

Portrait of Leonardo, age 60 — {{PD-1923}}

The next seven years would take a massive toll on Leonardo, both physically and mentally. At a time in life when he should be enjoying the fruits
of his labors, Leonardo entered the unhappiest episode of his life. He
emerged on the other side old and fragile, but his mind undimmed by the
body's trials.

FAMILIAR NAMES

Leonardo returned to the city of Milan in early 1513, but only briefly. For
the next several months he split his time between the city and the Melzi
villa in the country. In March of that year, strange news filtered in from
Florence. The summer before, it seems, the two surviving sons of Lorenzo
de'Medici — Giovanni and Guiliano — had returned from 18 years in ex-
ile to take control of Florence once more. By 1513, the political landscape
of northern Italy looked surprisingly familiar to Leonardo: Sforza in Milan
and Medici in Florence.

It had been more than 30 years since Leonardo had last been under the
protection of a Medici, but in the spirit of déjà vu, he received a letter from
Guiliano de'Medici sometime in the summer of 1513. Just a few months
before, Giovanni de'Medici, the eldest brother and a Cardinal in the Catholic Church, ascended to the throne of St. Peter to become Pope Leo X.
Giuliano took over the job of captain of the Pope's army, and a nephew of
the family was placed in charge of Florence.[127] Their power secured, Giuliano now requested the skill of Leonardo da Vinci, the wayward son of
Florence.

On September 24, 1513, Leonardo set out for Rome and — at least he
hoped — a chance to once more freely pursue his studies. And, of course,

---

127. Chambers, David. *Popes, Cardinals and War: the Church Militant in Early Modern
and Renaissance Europe*. Tauris, 2006. Print, 134-135.

he wanted to receive the praise that was his due. Accompanying him on this journey were the usual characters: Salai, Melzi and an assortment of apprentices. Paying 13 ducats in fees, Leonardo loaded 500 pounds of artwork, clothes, tools, and knick-knacks he had acquired over the years onto a carriage, bound for Rome.[128]

THE ETERNAL CITY

Although Leonardo had made a few brief visits to the city, including his short vacation in 1501, he had never lived in Rome before. No doubt, he still remembered Lorenzo de'Medici overlooking him for the position of painter-ambassador to the Pope those many decades ago. Now, he had arrived at the invitation of Lorenzo's son. The city of Rome was much smaller than Milan, with a population around 50,000. Its history, however, was far older, and Leonardo had enjoyed touring the ancient ruins of the Romans when he had visited the city previously. With each new Pope came building projects and improvements, so there always seemed to be some sort of construction going on. Rome looked like an up-and-coming city, always in flux. Underlying everything in the "eternal city," as Rome was called, was an insidious rot. Here, the positions of cardinals, princes, and Popes could be bought, sold, and traded. For all its being the heart of the Church, Rome was a rotten pit of debased morals and corruption, a place where people literally stabbed each other in the backs to get ahead. At 60, Leonardo was entering an arena that even a young man would find hard to survive.

It all began well enough. Giuliano housed Leonardo and his household in the Villa Belvedere, the summer Palace of the Pope. With huge, ancient, and half-wild gardens hidden among the spacious rooms, the Belvedere

---

128. Nicholl, Charles. *Leonardo Da Vinci: Flights of the Mind.* New York, NY: Penguin, 2005. Print, 459.

gave Leonardo plenty of fuel for his imagination. The first few weeks in Rome were also a time for Leonardo to reacquaint himself with some old friends who happened to be in the city. He met up with Atalante Migliorotti, the musician who had accompanied Leonardo on his first trip from Florence to Milan in 1482. Where there were old, fond, acquaintances, however, there were also old enemies. Working as the Pope's go-to artist, Michelangelo swaggered around town like a puffed up bird. He wasn't the only young artist who had crept into the limelight while Leonardo basked in the praises of the French. Foremost among them was Raphael, the Pope's favorite painter.[129]

What, then was Leonardo da Vinci? This would be a question that would nag Leonardo the entire time he stayed in Rome. Back in Milan, he had had little to no real competition — his fame as a painter, engineer, scientist, and all-around thinker was second to none. He was, however, a big fish in a little pond. Rome, although physically smaller than Milan, represented the center of power and fame in Italy. Leonardo would have no major painting commissions — in fact his career as a painter lay behind him, as he would later find out. A man who, whether he had liked it or not, had built his career on his skill as a painter, now found himself in a city full of them and all the great jobs already secured. After very little time at all, Leonardo looked around and discovered that the grand rooms and exotic gardens of the Belvedere acted more as a prison than as a symbol of esteem.

If he needed any more proof of this, all he had to do was look at his wages. Giuliano paid Leonardo a mere 33 ducats a month — a wage that was split between Leonardo and his assistants, who the artist had to pay. In comparison, the Pope paid Raphael 12,000 ducats for each room he painted in the papal palace!

---

129. Bramly, Serge. *Leonardo: The Artist and the Man*. London: Penguin, 1994. Print, 383.

FRUIT FROM THE ROTTEN TREE

It was during this dark time that Leonardo wrote the enigmatic sentence "I medici me crearono edesstrussono," alternately translated as "the Medici made me and they destroyed me" or "doctors made me and they destroyed me." At this point in his life, Leonardo could have meant either one. Leonardo once wrote that people should "try to keep in good health. You will do so better if you avoid doctors." There is also evidence that during this time the aging artist started suffering from recurring bouts of illness. Riddled among his notebooks at the time were addresses of local doctors and bits of advice on how to stay healthy.[130]

Don't Just Take my Word for It!

A few of Leonardo's tidbits of advice on healthy living include:

Do not eat when you have no appetite, and dine lightly,

Chew well, and whatever you take into you

Should be well cooked and of simple ingredients.

He who takes medicine is ill-advised,

Beware anger and avoid stuffy air.

Neither delay nor prolong your visits to the bathroom.[131]

But the Medici family, too, could have been the target of his frustration. Lorenzo played an important role in the beginning of Leonardo's career and, now, his son had enticed the artist to this wretched place at the end.

---

130. Ibid. 384.
131. Leonardo. *The Notebooks of Leonardo Da Vinci, Complete*. Trans. Jean Paul Richter. Dover Publications, Inc., 1972. Electronic. 437.

Whatever his meaning, it is clear from his writing that Leonardo was in a dark place. His depression revealed itself to others in a series of bizarre practical jokes the aging artist played on those around him. Giorgio Vasari provides us with the first of these somewhat harmful pranks:

> *"When the gardener of the Belvedere found a very odd-looking lizard, Leonardo attached wings to its back with a mixture of quicksilver [mercury]; they were made from scales stripped from other lizards and they quivered as it walked along. He gave the creature eyes, horns and beard, and then he tamed it, and kept it in a box to show his friends and frighten the life out of them."[132]*

Another of his "jokes" involved the stomach of a cow, which he had friends or visitors to the Belvedere hold in their hands. Attached to the stomach, however, was a tube whose other end connected to bellows hidden in another room. While his friends held the stomach, Leonardo would pump air into it so that it grew to such size that it filled the space of the entire room, forcing the friend to seek shelter from the billowing organ. These creepy pranks speak just as loudly about Leonardo's mindset as his strange sentence about doctors or the Medici.

In the absence of any clear commissions or jobs, Leonardo spent his time in Rome in pursuit of knowledge. He theorized and wrote pages on geometric equations, he made experiments on the way sound travels through the air, and he left the stifling confines of the city for the countryside as often as he could.[133] He once more returned to mechanics and designed machines for making rope and minting coins. He even painted a little, although not on the scale, or for the caliber of clients, as he had done in years

132. Vasari, Giorgio. *The Lives of the Artists*. Trans. Julia C. Bondanella and Peter Bondanella. New York: Oxford UP, 1991. Print, 296.
133. Nicholl, Charles. *Leonardo Da Vinci: Flights of the Mind*. New York, NY: Penguin, 2005. Print, 464.

past. Although he kept himself busy, and even produced a few books on his experiments and thoughts, trouble continued to plague Leonardo.

PAPAL TROUBLES

When Giuliano left Rome, which he frequently did, Leonardo was left flapping in the wind. It was Giuliano, not his brother the Pope, who asked Leonardo to Rome in the first place. Pope Leo X was a plump man — some even called him obese — who took advantage of all the pleasures his good life had to offer. He loved card games, hunting, music, and the company of clowns and jesters.

He did not like Leonardo.

After seeing the paintings Leonardo had made for one of his notaries, Pope Leo X asked Leonardo to paint him something as well. Here was Leonardo's chance, an opportunity to dazzle the man with all the money and power in Rome. If he could get an in with the Pope, then he might be able to turn around this depressing stay in the eternal city. Unfortunately, it was not to be. Leonardo made the mistake of preparing the varnish that he would apply to the work at the end before he even began the painting. Seeing this, Leo X scoffed: "here is a man, alas, who will never do anything since he is thinking of the completion of his painting before he has started."[134] In defense of Leonardo, he frequently started a project while already envisioning the end. A few years earlier he had written: "Think carefully about the end. Consider first the end." That was not a motto the Pope could get behind, and Leonardo stopped the painting immediately.[135]

134. Vasari, Giorgio. *The Lives of the Artists*. Trans. Julia C. Bondanella and Peter Bondanella. New York: Oxford UP, 1991. Print, 297.
135. Bramly, Serge. *Leonardo: The Artist and the Man*. London: Penguin, 1994. Print, 388.

His relationship with the Pope hit rock bottom when Leonardo took on an apprentice who had a nasty habit of spreading rumors. Frustrated at Leonardo for some perceived insult, this apprentice spread the rumor that Leonardo was a necromancer — a practitioner of the dark arts. Why else would a man take dead bodies and cut them into pieces, all the while scribbling notes on paper? Leonardo had indeed been continuing his study of human anatomy, using the hospital of San Spirito in the city for his supply of cadavers. With the cloud of witchcraft over his head, however, he had to immediately end what had become one of his favorite studies.[136]

Frustrated right and left, unable to carve out a place for himself in the crowded city of Rome, Leonardo had a frustrating two years.

RECONCILIATION

For all his challenges, Rome was not a complete waste of time for Leonardo. Quite unexpectedly, in 1514 he opened the door to find Giuliano di Ser Piero da Vinci — his half-brother. Giuliano da Vinci had led the charge against Leonardo during the fight over their uncle Francesco's will. Leonardo had never expected to see him again, yet here he was. Now in his mid-30s, a husband and father, Giuliano was in Rome on some business with the papal offices. He had come to Leonardo to patch things up. And to get some help.

Contacts were everything in Renaissance Italy — a lesson Leonardo had learned early while just starting out in Florence. Over the years, he had successfully made important connections to men throughout Europe. These contacts were what Giuliano needed. More specifically, he needed Leonardo to write on his behalf to the papal advisor in order to smooth out a business deal. Giuliano, like his father, was a notary. Perhaps because he

---

136. Ibid. 387.

felt so isolated and alone in Rome, faced with failure on nearly every front, Leonardo was eager to help his brother. Although we don't know the outcome of Giuliano's business deal, his reconnecting with Leonardo paved the way for a wider reconciliation between the artist and the rest of his family. While they may not have become the best of friends, at least Leonardo was given the chance to leave things with his father's family on good terms.[137]

A WAY OUT

With Leonardo patching things up with his family, his spirits might have been lifted going into 1515. Unfortunately, things would get worse for the artist before they got better. The recurring bouts of illness he kept suffering from appear to have culminated and caused a serious crisis the summer of 1515. Although we don't know the specifics of the illness, it is possible Leonardo da Vinci suffered a stroke. At 63-years-old, the great artist — the man who had created exceptional works of art with nothing but his hands — became partially paralyzed. He would never regain use of his right hand, and it is possible that the stroke affected other parts of his body. The one blessing he could salvage from this disaster was that at least he maintained complete control of his left hand — his dominate hand. Nevertheless, this stroke marked the end of Leonardo's career as a painter. Although he was still able to produce the same flawless drawings after the illness, the loss of mobility prevented him from taking on any large-scale projects like paintings. For a man who had filled his life with constant movement and activity, this blow from fate proved the most debilitating.

While recovering from the stroke, Leonardo's mind did what it had always done — it turned inwards. Reflecting his dark mood, Leonardo threw

---

137. Nicholl, Charles. *Leonardo Da Vinci: Flights of the Mind.* New York, NY: Penguin, 2005. Print, 465.

himself into the contemplation of a cataclysmic storm, like the one that drowned the world and necessitated the construction of Noah's Ark in the Bible. He filled pages and pages with drawings of storms, descriptions of violently falling water, and advice on how to capture their fury in drawings and paintings. His mood understandably depressed, his thoughts turned dark.[138]

Don't Just Take my Word for It!

Leonardo describes the deluge in these cataclysmic terms:

"Broken trees loaded with people. Ships broken in pieces, smashed against rocks. Flocks of sheep; hailstones, thunderbolts, whirlwinds. People on trees which are unable to support them . . . and lightening from the clouds illuminating everything."[139]

Relief for Leonardo finally came in the form of the French. As part of his role working for Giuliano, Leonardo accompanied him and the Pope on an important diplomatic mission in October of 1515. After kicking the French out of Italy as the head of the Holy League, the Pope now sought a means of securing peace. Meanwhile, yet another French king had died and a new one ascended the throne. The new king, François I, had just finished defeating the Sforza army near Milan when the Pope and his entourage — including Leonardo — arrived at the designated meeting site of Bologna in northern Italy.[140] At this point, Leonardo probably couldn't have cared less about the diplomatic proceedings. However, his decades of life as an artist

138. Nicholl, Charles. *Leonardo Da Vinci: Flights of the Mind.* New York, NY: Penguin, 2005. Print, 477.
139. Leonardo. *The Notebooks of Leonardo Da Vinci, Complete.* Trans. Jean Paul Richter. Dover Publications, Inc., 1972. Electronic. 268-270.
140. Chambers, David. *Popes, Cardinals and War: the Church Militant in Early Modern and Renaissance Europe.* Tauris, 2006. Print, 136-137.

in courts across Italy made him very aware of good opportunities. He saw a perfect opportunity in the 21-year-old François I. Immensely tall, with a long nose, François I was very charismatic. He was also a huge fan of Leonardo.

Ever since that first painting of *Madonna with a Yarn-Winder* found its way to the French capital, Leonardo had been a favorite of the royal family. His few years back in Milan under the patronage of the French governor had only solidified this reputation. For François I, Leonardo represented the best of Italy — forget all about the Michelangelos and Raphaels. There was only one Leonardo, and he surpassed everyone else. For Leonardo, François I represented the ideal life he had been missing in Rome. Although he had enjoyed the patronage of Ludovico Sforza back in the day, no prince in Italy had ever been able to lavish such money and praise on him like the sovereign of an entire kingdom; François I was security, freedom to pursue any and all studies, and an admirer — the very type of patron Leonardo was looking for. After all, everyone, especially an old man, loves to be doted on and respected.

François I proposed that Leonardo move to France, where he would be put up in a country villa and given as much money and comforts as he desired. There was no way he could refuse.[141]

FINAL TRIP

Leonardo, the bastard of a Florentine notary, born in the small town of Vinci, raised in Florence but a son of Milan, laid eyes on Italy for the last time in the autumn of 1516. He left behind Salai, his sometimes son, sometimes tormentor, at a piece of property he had been given years ago

---

141. Nicholl, Charles. *Leonardo Da Vinci: Flights of the Mind.* New York, NY: Penguin, 2005. Print, 485.

outside of Milan. Ascending the foothills of the Alps, Leonardo was joined by Melzi, who was then serving as his secretary, apprentice, and keeper of his notebooks. By the end of the year, Leonardo da Vinci resided in the manor-house of Cloux in the Loire Valley of France.

Officially, Leonardo was the king's "personal painter," but the stroke he had suffered made that an honorary title. After several years in Rome, beat down by depression and failure, Leonardo da Vinci arrived in France as a physically fragile man.

One visitor to the manor house remarked in his journal that Leonardo was a man of only 65 but looked many years older. Despite all of the health issues he had experienced lately, Leonardo's mind churned with just as much energy, thought up just as many innovative ideas and provided the man with just as many hours of delight as it had done when he was that young man in Florence.

Ultimately, it was his mind that the king found most attractive.

Don't Just Take my Word for It!

An eye witness remarked on the relationship between the king and his old Italian artist in this way:

> *"King François was completely besotted with those great virtues of Leonardo's, and took such pleasure in hearing him discourse that there were few days in the year when he was parted from him . . . I cannot resist repeating the words which I heard the King say of him. He said he could never believe there was another man born in this world who knew as much as Leonardo. And not only of sculpture, painting and architecture, and that he was truly a great philosopher."*

Later portrait of Leonardo looking haggard, possibly after suffering from a potential stroke and a period of depression — {{PD-1923}}

It might not be true to say that Leonardo knew more about the world than anyone living. However, the man possessed a broad and thorough understanding of such wide-ranging subjects that it could appear to be the case, especially from the perspective of a young king. With the same eloquence and charisma he had used to charm Ludovico Sforza those many years ago, Leonardo spent the last few years of his life in deep conversations with the king of France. When the king was pulled away from him, Leonardo took the opportunity to work with Melzi on the prodigious task of organizing his notebooks. By then, all his writings, doodles, drawings, and books made for a small library of material. Perhaps the best gift the king gave Leonardo in these final years was not the grand manor, or even the hefty salary, but the time and freedom to continue his thinking — on geometry, on machinery, on philosophy, and on art.

In April of 1519, Leonardo sat down with a notary to write his will. With no children, he dispersed the accumulated wealth and property he had acquired over the decades to those assistants and friends he was especially fond of. To Salai, Leonardo left the villa outside of Milan where the young man had been living the past few years. He even left some money to each of his brothers, since he had reconciled with them. To Giovanni Francesco Melzi, Leonardo left his legacy in the form of all his notebooks, all of his painting supplies, and all of the portraits and other paintings he still had — including the *Mona Lisa*.[142]

Leonardo di Ser Piero d'Antonio di Ser Piero di Ser Guido da Vinci died on May 2, 1519 at the age of 67 in the company of his dear Melzi.

---

142. Ibid. 498.

CHAPTER 11

Leonardo's Legacy

*T*hose closest to Leonardo da Vinci grieved his passing as family mourns the loss of a loved one. On June 1, 1519, just a month after Leonardo's death, Melzi wrote to Leonardo's half-brothers back in Italy with news of the great man's passing:

> *"He was like the best of fathers to me, and the grief that I felt at his death seems to me impossible to express; as long as there is breath in my body, I shall feel the eternal sadness it caused and with true reason, for he gave me every day proof of a passionate and ardent affection. Each of us must mourn the loss of a man such that nature is powerless to create another."[143]*

Leonardo had asked in his will to have a grand funeral and memorial, like the type of festivals that he had once enjoyed as a youth in Florence. For reasons that we no longer know, that did not happen. It took several months to finally lay him to rest in the local church in Amboise, France. We can imagine that Melzi was there, possibly even Salai since he would have had time to travel from Milan to France once news of Leonardo's death reached Italy. Leonardo's remains laid there in peace until 1802 when a French governor, at the insistence of Napoleon Bonaparte, tore down the chapel

---

143. Bramly, Serge. *Leonardo: The Artist and the Man.* London: Penguin, 1994. Print, 411-412.

and used the headstones to rebuild a country villa. Although he was unaware of it at the time, the bones he scattered and reburied in the corner of the cemetery contained the earthly remains of Leonardo da Vinci himself.

THE FATE OF HIS FRIENDS

Francesco Melzi did not immediately return to Italy. For several months after Leonardo's death, he remained in France on the payroll of the king — perhaps so that he could organize the wealth of material Leonardo had left him. In recognition of the king's support for Leonardo in his final years, Melzi left with the king all the paintings Leonardo had willed to him, including the *Mona Lisa*. In 1520, Melzi was back in Milan, carting with him the thousands of pages of notes, drawings, doodles, and thoughts: the physical legacy of Leonardo's great mind. For the rest of his life, which was a long one, Melzi curated this collection of material, displaying it in his house like a private library. He happily showed the work to any who wished to see it, including Giorgio Vasari, Leonardo's first biographer. Melzi died in 1570 at the age of 79.

The fate of Salai, Leonardo's little devil, was less happy. For a number of years he lived on the villa outside of Milan that Leonardo had willed him. In 1524, under circumstances that are now lost to history, Salai was killed by a bolt from a crossbow.

History has thankfully preserved the fate of Leonardo's other long-time friend and assistant Tommaso Masini, or "Zoroastro" as he was nicknamed. Oddly enough, in 1520 someone who had met Tommaso recorded that the strange man had with him "a serpent with four legs, which we take for a miracle; Zoroastro believes that some gryphon has carried it through the air from Libya [Africa]."[144] Could this be the strange lizard thing that Leon-

---

144. Nicholl, Charles. *Leonardo Da Vinci: Flights of the Mind.* New York, NY: Penguin, 2005. Print, 464.

ardo had created while in Rome? It would be in line with Tommaso's character to keep the strange oddity as a sort of keepsake years after Leonardo's death. Tommaso continued to practice his strange projects, which included alchemy and fortune-telling, in Rome and Florence and anywhere else he could find lodgings. Shortly after the 1520 reference to the strange lizard was noted, Tommaso Masini died.[145]

LEONARDO'S FAME

When he wrote his biography of the great artists of the Renaissance, which included a lengthy chapter on Leonardo, Giorgio Vasari set in stone the picture of Leonardo that the world would see for more than three centuries.

Don't Just Take my Word for It!

Vasari writes about Leonardo:

"Heaven sometimes sends us beings who represent not humanity alone but divinity itself, so that taking them as our models and imitating them, our minds and the best of our intelligence may approach the highest celestial spheres. Experience shows that those who are led by chance to study and follow the traces of these marvelous geniuses, even if nature gives them little or no help, may at least approach the supernatural works that participate in this divinity."

Translation: heaven sends up bright lights like Leonardo da Vinci so that we can bask in their magnificence and, it's hoped, attain some of that magnificence ourselves.

---

145. Ibid. 142.

Vasari's appraisal of Leonardo as a genius combined with all that remained of his paintings to create an odd legacy. Until the late 1800s when Leonardo's notebooks resurfaced and people began diving into the mind of the great man, Leonardo was primarily remembered as a master painter — and that's it. So for over three centuries, people largely ignored Leonardo's work in anatomy, geometry, mechanics, architecture, and philosophy. When people first started to look at his written words, they couldn't believe what they had been ignoring for so long. It was as if for the past 300+ years, the world had held a magnifying glass to one corner of the great tapestry that was Leonardo da Vinci's life. Only when his notebooks became public did the world set down the magnifying glass and see the true scope of Leonardo's genius.[146]

Over the course of the next 100 years, artists, writers, psychologists, and scientists delved into Leonardo's written record, pulling from it a wealth of information. Based on references Leonardo made in the notebooks that do survive, scholars estimate that we have fewer than two-thirds of the great man's notebooks. In 1965, an important portion of one of his books was discovered tucked away in stacks of the National Library in Madrid, Spain. There are potentially thousands of pages out there, hidden away in libraries or archives just like that.[147]

In the absence of any new discoveries, though, we are left to fill in the blanks of Leonardo's life with our own thoughts, hopes, and dreams. Where we cannot understand something, we invent it. This tendency has given rise to conspiracy theories about Leonardo da Vinci and groups like the Illuminati, Rosicrucians, and countless other secret societies. In our rush to untangle the untangleable, Leonardo has become what we want him to be.

---

146. Kemp, Martin. *Leonardo*. Oxford: Oxford UP, 2011. Print, 233.
147. Bramly, Serge. *Leonardo: The Artist and the Man*. London: Penguin, 1994. Print, 420.

He was a man "before his time," a genius who made the Renaissance, a conspirator, and whatever else we fancy him to be. I started this book with a question about who Leonardo da Vinci really was. In the spirit of Leonardo, I will leave this book unfinished, putting it to you, the reader, to answer that question yourself.

What is Leonardo da Vinci to you?

Author's Note

The first time I encountered Leonardo da Vinci was in 2008 when I visited the town of Vinci, Italy. I admit, that particular day I wasn't prepared to think about a man as complicated as Leonardo. The town was the third stop of the afternoon for the tour I was on. I was already tired, and the Italian summer sun suffocated what little energy I had remaining. What I remember most about that visit was the countryside. It took no imagination whatsoever to picture the sun-drenched hills with their rows of vineyards within sight of modern Vinci as Leonardo himself had seen them in the 1470s. Only the occasional asphalt highway snaking through the valley and the satellites perched on the red tile roofs of houses reminded you that you weren't in Renaissance Italy.

Today, the town of Vinci remains as a shrine to its favorite son. The museum of Leonardo da Vinci sits atop the most prominent hill in the community, dominating every line of sight. Everywhere you look, you are reminded that the great man himself was born here, grew up here, and returned here later in life. At the time, I was thankful to get back on the bus after an hour and a half in the sweltering sun. Now, however, I wish I had spent more time, just sitting and enjoying the very landscape that so enthralled Leonardo.

The second time I encountered Leonardo da Vinci, I was in graduate school studying for my Master of Arts degree in Art History and Archaeology.

While Renaissance art was not the focus of my degree, one of the faculty in the department was an expert in the subject. He would talk the ear off anyone willing to listen to him, not just about Leonardo, but about all the other artists of the period.

Researching and writing this book was the third time I encountered Leonardo da Vinci. Months spent reading about the man, pouring through his writings, and staring at his artwork has left me wanting more. Like everyone else, I want to fill in the blanks of his life with more detail. Unfortunately, we only have so many documents from that time, so the complete image of Leonardo will always be only half-finished.

Glossary

Accatabriga: Leonardo's stepfather

Albiera: Leonardo's first stepmother and Ser Piero's first wife. As a child, it is likely Leonardo was close to Albiera, who acted as a sort of mother

Altarpiece: A work of art, like a painting or sculpture, depicting a religious scene that hangs behind the altar in a church

Andrea Verrocchio: Leonardo's teacher and an important artist in his own right

Antonio di Ser Piero da Vinci: Leonardo's grandfather. Unlike the rest of the da Vinci men, Antonio was not a notary

Apprentice: A person learning a trade or skill from a skilled employer. Usually an apprentice has to pay the employer to learn the trade

Castello: Italian word for "castle"

Caterina: Leonardo's mother

Charles VIII, King of France: Invaded Italy in 1494 before being expelled from the area shortly thereafter

Compagnia di San Luca: The fraternity of painters Leonardo joined in Florence in 1472

Commission: A job or project. In Leonardo's case, he received commissions from wealthy individuals

Equestrian: Of or relating to a horse. Leonardo worked for years on the equestrian statue for Ludovico Sforza

Florin: A gold coin made in Florence. The Florin was often the coin of choice in Italy because of Florence's wealth and prestige in banking

Francesca da Vinci: Leonardo's second stepmother and Ser Piero's second wife. Leonardo likely had little contact with her since he only met her briefly before entering Andrea's studio as an apprentice

Francesco d'Antonio da Vinci: Leonardo's uncle. Only 15 years older than Leonardo, the two were very close

Gesso: A type of white paint artists used to coat wood panels before painting on them

Giorgio Vasari: An artist in his own right, Vasari wrote the book *The Lives of the Artists* about most of the important Renaissance artists in Italy. He was the first biographer of Leonardo. Although he never met Leonardo in person, Vasari was able to meet Melzi, Leonardo's good friend, and learn about the artist through him

Guild: Organizations created by and for people who worked in specific industries. There were guilds for bookkeepers, bankers, bakers and many others besides. These basically acted like professional clubs

Louis XII, King of France: Taking over the throne after Charles VIII, Louis XII successfully invaded Italy again in 1499, this time capturing Milan and Ludovico Sforza. This invasion forced Leonardo out of Milan after 18 years living in the city

Madonna: Another name of the Virgin Mary, Jesus' mother

Medici: A powerful Florentine banking family who ruled Florence from the mid-1400s through the mid-1500s with only a few breaks. Leonardo dealt mostly with **Lorenzo de'Medici** (also known as "il Magnifico" or "the Magnificent.") Lorenzo ruled Florence from 1469 until his death in 1492

Melzi, Giovanni Francesco: Leonardo's secretary and friend. When Leonardo died in 1519, Melzi inherited all of Leonardo's notebooks and his unfinished paintings. Melzi's care of these items allowed them to survive to this day

Mirror Script: Leonardo wrote in this style, writing from the right to the left and with letters that were backwards

Niccolò Machiavelli: A Florentine politician and author, Machiavelli is most famous for his books *The Prince* and *The Art of War*

Notary: Notaries were very important people in 14th and 15th century Italy. They were responsible for writing business and legal contracts and overseeing the creation of wills and other such documents. In a culture that thrived on business deals, a notary was a vital part of making the whole machine of state run smoothly

Patron: A person who gives financial or other support to a person. In Leonardo's case, his patrons were men like Ludovico Sforza and Charles d'Amboise, the French governor of Milan — individuals who continued to support the artist over a period of time

Pazzi Conspiracy: A failed overthrow of the Medici family, backed by the Pope in Rome and the Pazzi family in Florence. At the end of it, Lorenzo de'Medici's power was more secure than ever

Renaissance: Renaissance literally means "rebirth." It is a term used to describe the period of cultural growth that happened in Europe from the mid-14th century to the 17th century (1350 — 1600s). The height of the Renaissance took place in the 1400s-1500s.

Republic: A form of government where leaders act as representatives of the people who choose them

Salai: His real name was Giovanni Giacomo di Pietro Caprotti. As a young boy, he entered into the service of Leonardo and for the rest of Leonardo's life, the "little devil" would be a sort of son to him

Ser Piero d'Antonio da Vinci: Leonardo's father

Sforza: A Milanese family who ruled the city of Milan from the mid-1400s until the end of that century. **Ludovico Sforza** was the leader of Milan from 1476 until 1499. He was Leonardo's longest patron, giving the artist money, support and prestige for 18 years

Signoria: The name of the ruling council of Florence

Signore: The Italian name for Duke, or Prince. A few cities, like Milan, were ruled by a signore, whose heirs took over power when they died

Stylus: A type of pencil with which Renaissance artists used to draw

Tommaso di Giovanni Masini, "Zoroastro": Tommaso was an assistant of Leonardo's, off and on, for a number of decades. He sometimes served as a painting assistant, palm-reader and a number of other odd jobs

Vincio River: The river that gives the name to Leonardo's birth town, Vinci

Leonardo's Timeline

1452	Birth of Leonardo on April 15 in Vinci. Ser Piero, his father, marries Albiera
1457	Leonardo possibly living with his grandfather and grandmother alongside his uncle, Francesco
1464	Death of Albiera, Leonardo's first stepmother
1469	Death of Piero de' Medici, father of Lorenzo
1472	Leonardo becomes a member of the painters' fraternity in Florence
1473	First known drawing by Leonardo, possibly showing the landscape around Vinci
1478	The Pazzi Conspiracy rocks Florence and gives Leonardo his first taste of politics in Renaissance Italy
	Leonardo receives his first personal commission as an artist
1481	Leonardo is commissioned to paint an altarpiece by the friars at San Donato at Scopeto. He never finishes the piece.
1482	Leonardo leaves Florence for Milan
1483	Leonardo is commissioned to paint an altarpiece for a fraternity in Milan, to be displayed in a nearby church.
1485	Plague ravages Milan
1488	Andrea Verrochio, Leonardo's old teacher, dies
1490	While visiting Pavia, Leonardo studies the bronze sculpture there, taking notes for the design of his own equestrian statue for Ludovico Sforza
1492	Christopher Columbus sets sail on his voyage that ends in the discovery of the New World
1493	Leonardo's clay model of the Sforza horse statue is displayed in public
1494	French King Louis XII invades Italy. Ludovico Sforza allies himself with the invaders.

Leonardo's hopes of completing the Sforza horse statue are melted, along with the bronze that was going to be used for the statue.

1495	Leonardo begins the *Last Supper* in the refectory of the convent of Santa Maria della Grazie
1499	The French invade Milan, Ludovico Sforza is forced to flee.
1500	Leonardo leaves Milan after living there for 18 years and heads briefly to Mantua, then Venice and finally back to Florence
	Ludovico Sforza is captured by the French
1502	Leonardo becomes the military engineer of Cesare Borgia
1503–04	Leonardo leaves Cesare's service and returns to Florence
	Leonardo begins the *Battle of Anghiari*
1504	Ser Piero da Vinci, Leonardo's father, dies.
	Leonardo's uncle Francesco makes him his heir
1505	Possible second failed attempt at flight by Leonardo
1506	Leonardo leaves Florence to return to Milan, this time to work for the French
	Leonardo's uncle Francesco dies
1507–08	Leonardo meets Giovanni Francesco Melzi and begins dispute with his stepbrothers over Francesco's will
1508–09	Leonardo dives into the study of anatomy
1511	Leonardo's patron in Milan, Charles d'Amboise, dies and soldiers from the Holy League begin attacking French-controlled Milan
1512	The Medici take back power in Florence
1513	Leonardo moves to Rome at the request of Giuliano de'Medici, the son of Lorenzo de'Medici
1515	François I ascends to the throne of France and reconquers Milan
1516	Leonardo leaves Rome, and Italy, for the last time on his way to France
1519	On April 23 Leonardo makes his will. He dies on May 2.

Timeline of Paintings and Drawings

List of Leonardo's Paintings and Drawings that Exist Today[148]

Below are the paintings and important drawings almost certainly done by Leonardo himself. Several other works exist that are thought to have been painted by someone else but after a design made by Leonardo.

First Florentine Period

1472	Leonardo's first known drawing
1473–78	*Madonna of the Carnation*
1472–75	*The Annunciation*
1478–80	*Portrait of Genivra de'Benci*
1478–80	*Benois Madonna*
1480–82	*St. Jerome in the Wilderness* (unfinished)
1481–82	*Adoration of the Magi* (unfinished)

First Milanese Period

1483–85	*Virgin of the Rocks* (first)
1487–90	*Vitruvian Man*
1485	*Portrait of a Musician* (possibly)

---

148. All dates regarding Leonardo's work here and in the book are taken from Frank Zöllner's work, which is the most recent study of Leonardo's artistic work.

1489	*Lady with an Ermine* (Cecilia Gallerani)
1490-95	*Portrait of an Unknown Woman*
1492	Clay Model of Sforza Horse (all that remains are his drawings and sketches)
1495-97	*Last Supper*
1499-1500	*Virgin and Child with St. Anne* (unfinished drawing)

Second Florentine Period

1501-1507	*Madonna with a Yarn-Winder* (or *Madonna of the Yarnwinder*)
1503-1506	*Mona Lisa*
1503-06	*Battle of the Anghiari* (this only exists as drawings and sketches. Leonardo's half-finished painting of it in the Signoria's chambers was painted over 50 years after the artist's death by none other than Giorgio Vasari, the man who would be Leonardo's first biographer and an artist himself)

Second Milanese Period

1502-13	*Virgin and Child with St. Anne* (painting)

Rome Period

1513-1516	*St. John the Baptist*

Bibliography

Ady, Cecilia M. *A History of Milan under the Sforza*. N.p.: Methuen, 1907. Print.

Bartlett, Kenneth R. *A Short History of the Italian Renaissance*. Toronto: Toronto UP, 2013. Print.

Bramly, Serge. *Leonardo: The Artist and the Man*. London: Penguin, 1994. Print.

Brockwell, Maurice Walter. *Leonardo Da Vinci*. London: T.C & E.C. Jack, 1908. Electronic.

Burke, Peter. *The Italian Renaissance: Culture and Society in Italy*. Cambridge: Polity, 2014, Print.

Chambers, David. *Popes, Cardinals and War: the Church Militant in Early Modern and Renaissance Europe*. Tauris, 2006. Print.

Cohn, Samuel Kline. *The Laboring Classes in Renaissance Florence*. New York: Academic Press, 1980. Print.

Cruttwell, Maud. *Verrocchio*. New York: Charles Scribner's Sons, 1904. Print.

Fanelli, Giovanni. *Brunelleschi*. Firenze: Scala, 1980. Print.

Goldthwaite, Richard A. *The Building of Renaissance Florence: An Economic and Social History*. 1980. Print.

Hartley-Brewer, Julia. "Skydiver Proves Da Vinci Chute Works." The Guardian. Guardian News and Media, 27 June 2000. Web. 26 June 2017.

———— *History of Florence and the Affairs of Italy*. N.p.: Public Domain, 2001. Electronic.

Kemp, Martin. *Leonardo*. Oxford: Oxford UP, 2011. Print.

Leonardo. *The Notebooks of Leonardo Da Vinci, Complete*. Trans. Jean Paul Richter. Dover Publications, Inc., 1972. Electronic.

———— *Leonardo da Vinci: The Graphic Work*. Köln: Taschen, 2011. Print

Lubkin, Gregory. *A Renaissance Court: Milan Under Galeazzo Maria Sforza*. Berkeley: University of California Press, 1994. Print.

Machiavelli, Niccolo. *Mandragola*. Translated by Nerida Newbigin, Maryland: The Johns Hopkins UP, 2009. Elecronic.

McManus, I.C. "Life Expectation of Italian Renaissance Artists." *The Lancet*, Feb. 1, 1975. Electronic.

Najemy, John N. *A History of Florence: 1200-1575*. Massachusetts: Blackwell. 2008, Print.

Nicholl, Charles. *Leonardo Da Vinci: Flights of the Mind*. New York, NY: Penguin, 2005. Print.

Pedretti, Carlo. *The Literary Works of Leonardo da Vinci, Compiled and Edited from the Original Manuscripts by Jean Paul Richter*. Oxford: Phaidon, 1977, vol. 1. Print.

Potter, David. *Renaissance France at War: Armies, Culture and Society, C.1480-1560*. Boydell Press, 2008. Print.

"Signoria: Italian Medieval Government." *Encyclopedia Britannica.* 20 July 1998. Web. 20 Feb. 2017. Web.

Suh, H. Anna., ed. *Leonardo's Notebooks: Writing and Art of the Great Master.* New York: Black Dog & Leventhal, 2005. Print.

Vasari, Giorgio. *The Lives of the Artists.* Trans. Julia C. Bondanella and Peter Bondanella. New York: Oxford UP, 1991. Print.

Zöllner, Frank et. al. *Leonardo da Vinci: The Complete Paintings.* Köln: Taschen, 2011. Print.

Index

About the Author

Antone Pierucci is an author and professional historian who has worked in museums, archives and archaeological excavations around the United States and the world. He currently lives in Stockton, California. You can learn more about him and his work by visiting www.antonepierucci.com.